Hope
in a
Ballet
Shoe

Hope
in a
Ballet
Shoe

A True Story

Michaela and Elaine DePrince

FABER & FABER

First published, as *Taking Flight: From War Orphan to Star Ballerina*, by
Alfred A. Knopf, an imprint of Random House Children's Books,
a division of Random House LLC, a Penguin Random House
Company, New York, in 2014

First published in the UK in 2015
by Faber & Faber Ltd
Bloomsbury House
74–77 Great Russell Street
London WC1B 3DA

Typeset by RefineCatch Limited, Bungay, Suffolk
Printed and bound by CPI Group (UK) Ltd, Croydon, CRO 4YY

A CIP record for this book is available from the British Library

ISBN 978–0–571–31446–1

FSC
www.fsc.org
MIX
Paper from
responsible sources
FSC® C101712

2 4 6 8 10 9 7 5 3 1

To Charles DePrince,
gentle and generous father and husband

Prologue
The Black Swan

I stand in the wings, dressed in a lush black tutu embellished with black feathers and blood-red flowers. A silver tiara studded with crystal rhinestones crowns my hair, which is pulled tightly back in a thick bun. One at a time I flex my feet at the ankles, extend my legs, and point my toes to check that the ribbons of my pointe shoes are tied and securely tucked. 'A professional ballerina never allows her ribbons to flop loose around her ankles,' one of my favourite teachers would warn me. A tiny smile twitches at the corners of my mouth as I remember that seven-year-old girl with her ribbons flying about.

A sense of unreality grips me. A professional ballerina . . . is that really me? It seems that just yesterday I was an orphan child, a small, dirty-faced pikin – hungry, frightened and clinging for dear life to a dream of becoming a ballerina. As Mabinty Bangura, I danced on my bare toes in the mud of the rainy season, disturbing the breeding mosquitoes, who would rise up in anger and bite me – bringing malaria.

My arms prickle with goose bumps. I rub them away, remembering my sister Mia once telling me, 'They're swan bumps, Michaela, not goose bumps.' Are my swan bumps caused by nervousness, the chilly Berkshire air in the Ted Shawn Theatre at Jacob's Pillow, or haunting memories?

Why should I be nervous? This isn't the first time I've danced the act-two pas de deux from *Swan Lake* onstage as Odile, the dark and cunning daughter of the evil sorcerer, Von Rothbart. But it is the first time I have danced it in front of such a large audience of critics and other dancers. They flock to Jacob's Pillow in June of each year to attend this renowned festival, and here I am about to make my entrance, the youngest professional ballerina among them, dancing a role that demands maturity and sophistication. I feel like an imposter.

The Black Swan is a seductress, tantalising Prince Siegfried with her womanly charms in order to steal him away from Odette, the White Swan. What do I know about womanly charms or seduction? After my April performance, one critic wrote, 'She was the sweetest seductress you ever saw . . . but she has yet to develop any ballerina mystique. She is only eighteen.' I showed the review to Skyler, my boyfriend. 'Do you agree?' I asked him, with tears in my eyes.

'She's right. You are sweet,' he answered.

'But I don't want to be sweet. I want to have womanly charms. I want to be a seductress. I want ballerina mystique.'

Skyler laughed and said, 'You're cute and funny too.'

'But I don't want to be cute and funny. I want to be mysterious.'

'Well, sometimes you're a complete mystery to me,' he admitted with a mischievous grin.

'That's not the same as ballerina mystique.'

Now it's the final performance of the season. I need to pull it off. For a brief second I am tempted to flee. Then the music starts, and I step onto the stage. Suddenly I am neither Mabinty Bangura, nor Michaela DePrince. I *am* the Black Swan, and as a reviewer later acknowledges, 'The vile Odile was delightfully chilly as she seduced the unwitting prince.'

Chapter 1

From the House on the Right

Before I was the 'vile' and 'chilly' Odile, I was Michaela DePrince, and before I was Michaela, I was Mabinty Bangura, and this is the story of my flight from war orphan to ballerina.

In Africa my papa loved the dusty, dry winds of the Harmattan, which blew down from the Sahara Desert every December or January. 'Ah, the Harmattan has brought us good fortune again!' he would exclaim when he returned from harvesting rice. I would smile when he said that because I knew that his next words would be, 'But not as good a fortune as the year when it brought us Mabinty . . . no, never as good as that!'

My parents said that I was born with a sharp cry and a personality as prickly as an African hedgehog. Even worse, I was a girl child, and a spotted one at that, because I was born with a skin condition called vitiligo, which caused me to look like a baby leopard. Nevertheless, my parents celebrated my arrival with joy.

When my father proclaimed that my birth was the

high point of his life, his older brother, Abdullah, shook his head and declared, 'It is an unfortunate Harmattan that brings a girl child . . . a worthless, spotted girl child at that, one who will not even bring you a good bride-price.' My mother told me that my father laughed at his brother. He and Uncle Abdullah did not see eye to eye on almost everything.

My uncle was right in one respect: in a typical household in the Kenema District of south-eastern Sierra Leone, West Africa, my birth would not have been cause for celebration. But our household was not typical. First of all, my parents' marriage had not been arranged. They had married for love, and my father refused to take a second wife, even after several years of marriage, when it appeared that I would be their only child. Secondly, both of my parents could read, and my father believed that his daughter should learn to read as well.

'If my brother is right and no one will wish to marry a girl with skin like the leopard, it is important that our daughter go to school. Let's prepare her for that day,' my father told my mother. So he began to teach me the *abjad*, or Arabic alphabet, when I was just a tiny pikin, barely able to toddle about.

'Fool!' Uncle Abdullah sputtered when he saw Papa moulding my little fingers around a stick of charcoal. 'Why are you teaching a girl child? She will think that she is above her station. All she needs to learn is how to cook, clean, sew and care for children.'

~

My spots scared the other children in our village. Nobody would play with me, except my cousins on occasion, so I would often sit alone on the stoop of our hut, thinking. I wondered why my father would work so hard panning for diamonds in the alluvial mines, diamonds that he would not be allowed to keep. It was hard, backbreaking work to stand bent over all day. Papa would hobble home at night, because his back, ankles and feet ached. His hands would be swollen and painful from sifting the heavy, wet soil through his sieve. Then, one night, while Mama was rubbing shea butter mixed with hot pepper into Papa's swollen joints, I overheard a conversation between them, and understood.

'It is important that our daughter go to school to learn more than we are capable of teaching her. I want her to go to a good school.'

'If we are frugal, the money from the mines will eventually be enough to pay her school fees, Alhaji,' my mother said.

'Ah, Jemi, count the money. How much have we saved so far?' Papa asked.

Mama laughed. 'This much, plus the amount I counted the last time you asked,' she said, holding up the coins he had brought home that evening.

I smiled a secret smile from my small space behind the curtain. I loved to listen to my parents' voices at night. Though I cannot say the same for the voices of Uncle Abdullah and his wives.

~

Our house was set to the right of my uncle's house. Uncle Abdullah had three wives and fourteen children. Much to his unhappiness, thirteen of his children were girls, leaving my uncle and his precious son, Usman, the child of his first wife, as the only males in the household.

Many nights I would hear cries and shouts of anger drifting across the yard. The sounds of Uncle Abdullah beating his wives and daughters filled my family with sadness. I doubted that Uncle Abdullah ever loved any of his wives, or he would not have beaten them. He certainly didn't love his many daughters. He blamed any and all of his misfortunes on their existence.

My uncle cared only about his one son. He called Usman his treasure and fed him delicious tidbits of meat while his daughters looked on, hungry and bloated by a starchy diet of rice and cassava, that long, brown-skinned root vegetable that lacks vitamins and minerals. And nothing was more galling to my uncle than finding me outside, sitting cross-legged on a grass mat, studying and writing my letters, which I copied from the Qur'an. He could not resist poking me with the toe of his sandal and ordering me to get about the duties of a woman.

'Fool!' Uncle Abdullah would sputter at my papa. 'Put this child to work.'

'What need does she have of womanly chores? She is only a child herself,' Papa would remind his brother, and then couldn't resist adding: 'Yes, not even four years old, and yet she speaks Mende, Temne, Limba, Krio and Arabic. She picks up languages from the marketplace and learns quickly. She will surely become a scholar.' Papa didn't need to rub any more salt in Uncle Abdullah's wounds by reminding him that Usman, who was several years older than me, lagged far behind me in his studies.

'What she needs is a good beating,' Uncle Abdullah would counter. 'And that wife of yours, she too needs an occasional beating. You are spoiling your women, Alhaji. No good will ever come of that.'

Perhaps Papa should not have bragged about my learning. The villagers and my uncle thought that I was strange enough with my spots, and my reading made me even stranger in their eyes and made my uncle hate me.

The only thing that my father and his brother had in common was the land that fed us, sheltered us, and provided the rice, palm wine and shea butter that we sold at the market.

At night, when I heard the cries coming from across the yard, I'd turn my ear towards my parents resting on the other side of the curtain. From there I heard sweet words of love and soft laughter. Then I would thank Allah because I had been born into the house on the right, rather than the one on the left.

Chapter 2

To the House on the Left

A civil war had started in my country in 1991, and by the time I was three years old, it had been going on for seven years. It had begun mainly because the education system shut down, and without schooling, young people could not get jobs. This resulted in poverty and hunger, which made them desperate, so they formed a revolutionary army to fight for what they needed.

As the war progressed, the youth lost track of their goals and started killing innocent villagers. So now, instead of good luck, the dry season brought an invasion of rebels of the Revolutionary United Front. They called themselves the RUF, but their victims combined the English words *rebel* and *devil*, and called them *debils*.

~

The Harmattan that my father had always loved betrayed us that year. Instead of good luck, it brought the war to our village. Papa was not at home the day the debils burned the rice and palm trees that grew on the nearby hillsides. He was at the diamond mines. When he got home, Mama would need to tell him that the debils left us with no crop to sell, no rice to eat, and no seed for next year's planting.

Mama and I sat on a wooden bench at the front of our home and watched the flames that were being spread by the strong Harmattan winds. The smoke made it difficult to breathe. I sobbed and coughed, and she wrapped her arms around me. 'Mama, why aren't you crying?' I asked.

Mama pointed towards another village on the hillside. I could see smoke rising from the homes there. 'We are fortunate that the debils spared our homes and our lives,' she answered. 'We should be grateful to Allah for that.'

Maybe she was right, but I didn't feel grateful. A few minutes later, a man came to our door, moaning and wailing. He told us that he was the only survivor of his village. The debils had forced him to watch as they killed his friends and family. Then, laughing, they asked if he preferred short sleeves or long sleeves. He said that he usually wore long sleeves, so they cut off his hand and sent him on his way to spread fear and warnings throughout the countryside.

Auntie Yeabu, the youngest wife of Uncle Abdullah,

helped my mother bandage the man's stump while I stood nearby, shaking with fear. Mama offered the man the small portion of rice remaining from our morning meal. She begged him to rest in our house. But the man was certain that the debils would soon pass through our village, recognise him, and kill him too. So, instead of resting, he hurried north toward Makeni, a city many kilometres away, where he thought it might be safe.

~

Mama scooped less rice than usual into the cook pot that night. I knew that she would barely eat any of it so that Papa and I could fill our bellies. I decided that I would follow her example. After working all day at the diamond mines, Papa would need the largest serving of rice.

While the rice bubbled in the pot, we continued to wait for him. Mama insisted that I eat. 'I want to wait for Papa,' I protested.

'No, you eat. I will wait,' Mama said. 'You are a growing child. Eat.'

'I'm not hungry,' I cried. I curled up next to her and fell asleep.

~

I woke up to the sound of my cousin Usman's voice. 'Auntie Jemi,' he hissed quietly. 'Auntie Jemi, the rebels came to the mines today. They shot all of the workers.'

'All of the workers?' my mother repeated. 'And Alhaji?'

'Yes, Uncle Alhaji too,' Usman whispered.

'NO-O-O!' I screamed. 'Not Papa!'

'NO-O-O!' Mama screamed. 'Not my Alhaji!'

Mama and I clung tightly to each other. She rocked me in her arms as I cried loudly.

Soon the entire village was filled with weeping, because nearly every family lost a father, brother, son or nephew. On the day my father died, I believed that I was feeling the worst pain possible . . . that I would never again feel such pain. Then I moved into the house on the left and learned that pain, like the green of the jungle leaves, comes in many shades.

~

Uncle Abdullah decided to rent our house to a refugee family and forced Mama and me to move into his house. According to Sharia, Muslim law, Uncle Abdullah became our guardian. He took the money my parents had saved for my education, and because we had no money left, Mama and I could not escape. My uncle wanted to marry Mama, but Sharia also gave her the right to refuse his offer, which she did. Her rejection enraged him, and he would use any excuse to punish us.

Mama and I lived in constant fear of him. I'll never forget him shouting at us, 'You are punished! No food for either of you! No food today, tomorrow, and the day after that!'

Auntie Yeabu often tried to sneak food to us, but she wasn't always able to do so, because my other aunts' eyes were too sharp. We often went hungry, and for months Mama gave me most of her food. 'I'm not so hungry today. You eat my rice,' she would say to me. I didn't believe her, so I would try to refuse it, but she insisted. 'I will throw it away if you don't eat it,' she'd threaten. Tears would fill my eyes, and even though I was very hungry, the rice would form a lump in my throat as I tried to force it down.

I know now that Mama was starving and gave me her rice so that I would not starve with her. Yet, even with her food, my face swelled and my belly stuck out, something that often happens to starving children.

Uncle Abdullah would yell at me. 'You are a useless child! Look at you. How ugly you are. You have the spots of a leopard. I am wasting food and money on you. I will not even get a bride-price in return. Who would want to marry a girl who looks like a dangerous beast of the jungle?'

Oh, how I hated my uncle then. I wanted to shout back at him, but I didn't dare. Instead I ran to my mother and curled up in her arms.

Chapter 3

When the Rain Came

The dry season seemed to last for ever the year that my father died, making food even more scarce. I breathed a sigh of relief when I awoke early one morning and smelled the scent of rain in the air. Clouds were forming on the horizon. *Ah, the wet season will soon be here, and fruit will grow wild on the trees, and the animals in the bush will grow fat,* I told myself.

I couldn't wait to tell Mama, but she was sleeping peacefully, and I didn't want to wake her. She had been sick for several days. The night before she had vomited so much that she had a nosebleed.

Most of the night I had heard Mama tossing and turning. Just before dawn I heard her sigh loudly three times and finally grow quiet. I smiled to myself, relieved that she was asleep. I brought out my father's notebook and pen, and started to write, knowing that when Uncle Abdullah awoke, I would need to hide them again.

Eventually everyone else got up, leaving only Mama and Uncle Abdullah asleep. I started to worry. If Uncle

Abdullah awoke and found my mother asleep, she would be beaten again. Worse yet, he wouldn't give her any more food. When I heard my uncle, I leaped from my grass mat and hurried to her.

'Mama! Mama, wake up,' I urged as I shook her shoulder. 'Uncle Abdullah will beat you if you do not wake up. Please, Mama! Please, Mama!' I begged over and over again as I shook her harder and harder.

Auntie Huda rushed over and saw blood on Mama's face. 'How long has Jemi been sick?' she asked Auntie Yeabu.

'Days,' Auntie Yeabu responded.

'Fool!' Auntie Huda yelled. 'She has Lassa fever.' She looked at me strangely and asked her sister wives, 'Has the spotted devil child been sick too?'

Auntie Yeabu shook her head no, too frightened to speak.

Auntie Huda banished me to the yard. I ran outside and crouched close to the doorway, listening to them argue about Lassa fever.

Maybe the refugees who piled into the refugee camps close by had carried it. Maybe Auntie Huda was right, and my mother had been asking for trouble when she helped the man with the missing hand.

'Mama!' I called from the doorway. 'Please, may I come in?'

Auntie Yeabu slipped away from the other wives and

came to me. She picked me up and covered my eyes with her *lapa*, the long colourful scarf that was wrapped around her and lay across her shoulder. I pushed the *lapa* away, but Auntie Yeabu said, 'No, leave it. You don't want to see them carrying off your mother's body to be buried.'

Until that moment I had not realised that my mother was dead. Suddenly I was overwhelmed by the thought that she was gone for ever. I began to scream. Grief-stricken, I sobbed, 'Please! Please! I want to be with my mama! Bury me too! I don't want to be alive! Nobody loves me!'

'Hush!' Auntie Yeabu begged. 'I wouldn't put it past Abdullah to toss you into the grave with your mother.' But I couldn't be quiet. I cried and howled while she held me even tighter for fear that I would jump into the hole that Uncle Abdullah and the village men had dug.

Finally I escaped Auntie Yeabu's clutches as they tossed shovelfuls of dirt over my mother's body, but I was too late. I broke my fingernails as I tried to claw my way through the dirt to her, but Uncle Abdullah grabbed me and tossed me towards his wives. 'Control this crazy child!' he roared.

After my mother was buried, Uncle Abdullah burned her belongings, afraid that they had been tainted by the fever. Now I had nothing to remember her by.

Uncle Abdullah turned away from my tear-stained

face. He had only one concern. He asked, 'What will I do if Usman catches this disease?' Then he checked all of my cousins for signs of Lassa fever.

'Mabinty brings us nothing but trouble. It is the spots,' Uncle Abdullah's first wife mumbled to her sister wives. 'That and her reading. Only a devil child can read when so young. She has brought nothing but bad luck to this family. It is time to be rid of her.'

~

I was used to having my mother sleep close to me at night. She would wrap her arms around me and sing me to sleep, her voice carrying me to a place where I could forget my misery. Without her, I tossed and turned until my uncle nudged me with his foot and said, 'Get your belongings, and follow me.'

I had no idea where he was planning to take me, but I knew that I would want my writing notebook and pen wherever I was going. I hid them in a piece of cloth and tied it around my chest under my dress. I patted myself, satisfied that they were flat enough so that my uncle would not notice them. Then I rolled up the grass mat my mother had woven for me and lifted it onto my shoulder.

I followed Uncle Abdullah down the winding road of orange dirt that ran past our home. 'Where are we going?' I asked in a voice hoarse from crying. Uncle Abdullah grunted in response only, so I didn't give him the satisfaction of asking again, but I couldn't stop my tears. I missed my parents, and without them by my side, I feared what the future would bring.

Soon we started seeing more and more people on the road, travelling with their meagre belongings on their heads. Uncle Abdullah spoke with them, and I learned that they were walking the 147 kilometres to Makeni in order to escape the debils.

'Won't the debils just follow everyone to Makeni?' I asked, hiccoughing from so much crying, but Uncle Abdullah ignored my question, and with his walking stick, he poked at my legs, prodding me to walk faster.

'Your daughter looks tired. If you wish, she may climb into my cart,' a ragged man on the road said. 'I will only charge you a small amount ... only five leones.'

Uncle Abdullah snorted. 'I will not pay even one leone. She can walk ... and she isn't my daughter,' he answered gruffly, clearly insulted by the man's assumption that he had fathered such an ugly child.

Uncle Abdullah and I followed the flow of people to Makeni. Suddenly, the sky rumbled and the clouds burst. The thunder drowned out my sobs, and the raindrops mixed with my tears.

I held my bundle closer to my chest as I plodded

through the mud, which sucked at my rubber sandals. Finally the mud swallowed my right sandal. I walked with one sandal and one bare foot, but soon the mud claimed my second sandal too.

Most of the walkers took shelter under the trees and brush, but Uncle Abdullah and I walked on and on. Then a lorry stopped, and a voice called out. Uncle Abdullah's face lit up when he recognised Pa Mustapha, a friend from the marketplace. The friend beckoned Uncle Abdullah over to the lorry and said something to him.

Suddenly Uncle Abdullah picked me up and threw me into the open bed of the lorry, where I landed in the several inches of rainwater that sloshed at the bottom. Then he climbed into the dry cab.

The lorry bounced down the road towards Makeni, and I bounced with it as I wrapped myself in my grass mat and continued to cry for the loss of all my happiness. Eventually I fell sound asleep, hungry, wet and sadder than I had ever felt before.

Chapter 4

At the Orphanage

The rain had stopped, and the last rays of the sun were disappearing when I awoke. Uncle Abdullah opened the tailgate of the lorry and crooked his finger to beckon me out. Then he tipped his nose in the direction of a gate without saying a word to me. I stared at a large sign, but it wasn't in Arabic, so I couldn't read it.

I hopped out and followed him without argument. 'My mat! Wait!' I shouted to Pa Mustapha, but he was gunning the motor and didn't hear me. He pulled away before I could hop back up and get my grass mat.

Uncle Abdullah gave me a shove towards the gate, not caring that I had lost my only remaining connection to my mother. Out of nowhere, a girl appeared from behind the gate. She crouched down and stared at us. 'Don't just sit there staring,' Uncle Abdullah grumbled at her. 'Go and find the director,' he ordered.

The girl leaped to her feet, ran to a nearby building, and called out, 'Papa Andrew! A man and a pikin are here to see you.'

A man in tan pants, a blue shirt and brown shoes with laces came out of the building. 'Welcome to the Safe Haven Orphanage,' he said. Then he introduced himself to Uncle Abdullah as Andrew Jah, the director of the orphanage.

My head jerked up, and I stared at the man. Had I heard him correctly? Had he said 'orphanage'? Was I now nothing more than an orphan? I had no one to love me or protect me . . . no one to think that I was special. These thoughts tumbled through my mind as I heard my uncle explain, 'My brother has been killed. His wife recently died. I bring you my young niece, their daughter. I am her guardian, but I cannot care for her. I have three wives and many children of my own, so I cannot waste food on her. Besides, she is an ugly, sharp-tongued, evil-tempered child with spots. I will never get a bride-price for her. I am sure you understand.'

Andrew Jah crouched before me and asked, 'What is your name?'

'Mabinty Bangura,' I promptly answered.

'What language do you speak?' the director asked in Krio.

When I hesitated, Uncle Abdullah swatted my head, and Andrew Jah began to ask the same question in Mende, but I interrupted him in Krio, saying, 'I speak Krio, Mende, Temne, Limba and Arabic.'

'So many languages for such a small pikin!' Andrew Jah exclaimed.

'I learned them in the market when I helped my parents in their stall.'

At that very moment, my papa's pen fell from under my dress and landed at the director's feet. When I tried to retrieve it, the tie around my chest loosened and the notebook slipped out too.

'What is this you were carrying under your dress?' Andrew Jah asked, pointing his nose towards my bundle.

I carefully unwrapped the cloth from around the notebook, relieved to discover that it was not too wet, and held it out to the director with shaking hands. He took the notebook from me and carefully turned the pages. 'What have we here?' he asked with surprise.

'It is my notebook,' I answered quietly, afraid he would take it away.

'And who did all of this?' He pointed to the writing.

'I did.'

'Do you mean to tell me that you are only four, yet you can read and write Arabic?' the director asked, startled.

I nodded my head, and he looked at my uncle and said, 'This child shows great promise. Our orphanage is full, but I will make room for her under one condition. You cannot return to claim her.'

'I have no intention of doing that,' Uncle Abdullah said. 'I am glad enough to be rid of her.'

Then the man invited us into a small room where he gave my uncle some papers to sign. The papers were in English, which my uncle could not read, so the man read them to him and translated them into Krio as I waited quietly and listened carefully. Many of the words were too complicated for me to understand, but I did get the gist of the papers' content. They said that I would be educated and sent to live with a family in another country.

'What other country?' Uncle Abdullah asked.

'The United States of America,' Andrew Jah answered, and then he showed my uncle where to sign his name. My heart beat loudly at the words *United States of America*. The name of that country had been special to my parents. They had often spoken of someday taking me there. 'It is a place where education is free – even for girls!' my papa had said.

When the director saw that Uncle Abdullah did not know how to sign his name, he removed a small black pad from his drawer, rolled my uncle's thumb on the pad, and pressed it onto the paper, leaving a neat thumb print on the document. 'Now I can prove that you were in agreement with me,' Andrew Jah said.

'How much will you be paying me for the child?' Uncle Abdullah asked.

'We do not pay for children. The fact that we will feed them, care for them, educate them and find them a good home is payment enough to most parents,' the director said.

'I am not her parent. My own children are not spotted, like her,' Uncle Abdullah retorted. He snatched the thumb-printed paper away. 'I could just as easily sell her to a cocoa plantation,' he shouted as he seized my arm and began dragging me through the door.

I grabbed the door frame and held on tightly. I wanted to go to the United States of America, but my uncle was big and strong, so he pried me away with little difficulty. I bit him, clinging to his leg with my teeth like a rabid dog. 'Wait!' Andrew Jah cried out, interceding. He coaxed my teeth off my uncle. Then he said the words that Uncle Abdullah so obviously longed to hear: 'I have some money for you. We do not ordinarily pay for children, but we sometimes help their families when they are in need.' He unlocked a metal drawer in a cabinet and removed some paper money. He held it out to my uncle.

'Ah yes. This will help me feed my hungry family,' Uncle Abdullah said as he fondled the bills. Then he turned on his heel and left me behind without as much as a goodbye. I wasn't sad to see him go, but I would miss some of my cousins and Auntie Yeabu. I hadn't even been allowed to say goodbye to them.

The director placed his hand on my shoulder and said, 'You will call me Papa Andrew now, because in this place I'll be your papa. Do you understand?'

My stomach did flip-flops. It made me feel sick to call this strange man Papa. Before I could answer him, the director turned me over to a woman he called Auntie Fatmata, a village woman who worked and lived at the orphanage. Her mouth was turned down in a frown. She rolled her eyes at me and grunted. I could tell that she didn't like me.

When Auntie Fatmata saw me hopping from foot to foot, she led me to an outbuilding with toilets, which were really only holes in the ground, covered with a wooden plank. She told me to be careful, because children had occasionally fallen into the holes. 'And watch out for the snakes,' she warned. Then she laughed and walked out, leaving me alone in the darkness.

When I finished in the outhouse, Auntie Fatmata was waiting outside for me. She walked me to a building near Papa Andrew's office. It contained a large room where many girls slept two by two on grass mats upon the floor. Auntie Fatmata pointed to a mat where one girl sat, as though awaiting my arrival. She was the girl from the gate.

I was about to say, 'I have my own mat, woven by my mother,' when I remembered that I had left it behind in the lorry. I felt a sudden pang in my chest. That mat had been my only link with my mother, and I had lost it. I dropped, like a limp doll, onto the girl's mat, shivering in my wet clothes.

My shoulders shook as I began to sob into my arms.

'Hush, hush,' the girl beside me whispered. 'If you awaken Auntie Fatmata with your crying tonight, she will beat you with her willow switch.'

The thought of a beating caused me to cry harder. The girl began to pat my back and sing softly, just like my mother would do whenever I had a bad dream. The girl's sweet voice slowly lulled me into a surprisingly sound sleep.

Chapter 5

Number Twenty-Seven

Bright sunlight streamed through the window and into my eyes, awakening me. 'Mama . . . Papa,' I whispered, and then I remembered. They were gone. My home was gone. The life I had known was gone. I was sleeping in a room full of strangers in a strange place . . . an orphanage.

I rolled over and looked at the girl beside me. She was frowning. 'What's wrong?' I asked, thinking that, in the daylight, she had seen my spots and regretted sharing her mat with me.

She wrung her hands together as though she was afraid to tell me something. Then she whispered, 'I am so very sorry. I've wet the mat.'

I bolted upright and stared down at the mat. Sure enough, a dark stain spread over it. I bit my tongue, remembering how kind she had been to me the night before. 'It will dry,' I said as I helped her roll up the grass mat and carry it into the yard, where we spread it out to dry in the morning sun.

'Hurry,' the girl urged after we completed our chore. 'The aunties will soon be calling our numbers for breakfast.'

'What numbers?' I asked.

'You'll hear,' she said. Then she grabbed my hand and pulled me along behind her.

Outside, all of the other orphans gathered to wait for breakfast. They were chattering as loudly as the monkeys in a mango tree until I stepped into the sunny yard. Then they stopped and stared. I knew that they were staring at my spots. I looked down at the ground, ashamed.

'Don't look down,' my new friend said. 'Hold your chin up high.' Then she smiled at me, grabbed my hand, and pulled me towards the group.

Two aunties lugged a large cook pot into the yard. One stood over the pot with a ladle in her hand. 'That is Auntie Sombo. She isn't evil, just shy and a bit stupid,' my friend whispered. 'Auntie Fatmata . . . well, she is the evil one,' she explained as she gestured toward the tall, thin auntie who called out, 'Number One, Kadiatu Mansarey; Number Two, Isatu Bangura; Number Three, Sento Dumbaya . . .' On and on she went as she called up most of the twenty-four girls and three boys who lived at the orphanage.

Just then I realised that I didn't even know my new friend's name, but I was too scared to speak while the aunties spoke. I waited for her to step forward so that I could learn it. 'Number Twenty-Six, Mabinty . . .' I started to step forward, but my friend tugged at my dress, and I stopped in my tracks just as Auntie Fatmata called out the family name: 'Suma.' My new friend stepped forward to accept her bowl of rice. We had the same first name.

Finally the auntie called, 'Number Twenty-Seven, Mabinty Bangura.' I hurried to claim my food, and I immediately noticed that my bowl was not as full as most of the others had been. I looked at Mabinty Suma's bowl. Her bowl was only a bit fuller than mine, as was the bowl of Number Twenty-Five, Mariama Kargbo. I understood that it was not a good thing to be Number Twenty-Seven, because the rice ran out by the time the aunties got to the last girl.

When I turned with my bowl in my hands, I saw Mabinty Suma wave to me. 'Mabinty Bangura, come eat with me,' she said. I smiled because I had a friend. I had never had a friend before, just cousins.

I crouched down beside Mabinty Suma, and we began talking. Then she scooped up some of the rice with the fingers of her left hand and shovelled it into her mouth. I gasped. Everyone, even the youngest children, know that you eat with your right hand and toilet with your left hand.

Mabinty Suma looked up at me. Before I could even

utter a word, she said, 'I am Number Twenty-Six because I am left-handed . . . and because I wet my mat.' She added in a whisper, 'The aunties hate me more for my left-handedness than my bed-wetting. Other girls wet their beds because they are just as afraid as I am of wandering off to the toilet in the dead of night.'

Suddenly I realised that, as Number Twenty-Seven, *I* was the least-favoured child in the entire orphanage. No wonder I had received the smallest serving of rice! I felt the heat rise to my face. My spots were on fire. I thought that they were glowing so brightly that everyone would look at them.

Just then Auntie Fatmata noticed our mat. 'Look, Sombo, can you believe that Number Twenty-Six has peed on her mat yet again? Is she too lazy or too stupid to get up in the night and go to the toilets?'

Auntie Sombo grinned and bobbed her head in agreement. Some of the children grinned along with her, while others looked at their feet. I could tell just by looking at their faces which ones had left wet mats in the sleeping room. Surely Auntie Fatmata was smart enough to know that Mabinty Suma was not the only bed-wetter.

Auntie Fatmata grabbed her switch, and Mabinty Suma's eyes welled up with tears. 'Come here, Number Twenty-Six,' the auntie ordered.

Before thinking, I stepped forward and stood between Auntie Fatmata and Mabinty Suma. 'No, don't hit her. That is unfair. You know that she's not the only one to wet her sleeping mat.'

The auntie threw her head back and cackled. 'Listen to the ugly one, Sombo. This spotted child, the ugliest girl I have ever seen, thinks that she can tell me what to do.' Then Auntie Fatmata raised her switch and struck me first and then Mabinty Suma. She struck us over and over again, raising welts all over our bodies. Finally she said to me, 'Now you are striped as well as spotted.'

Mabinty Suma was crying loudly, but I was too angry to cry. My anger burned inside me like a fire. Papa had once read me a story about fire-breathing dragons. I wished that I were a dragon and could shoot out my anger in a breath of fire.

Later, while the other children played soccer, the aunties punished us by putting us to work feeding and bathing the babies. I liked babies, so I didn't mind this job at all. They were funny and sweet and didn't care that I had spots.

When the babies were clean and their bellies were full, we went back to the sleeping room with our grass mat. Just in time too, because the sky split open and the rain fell.

Once inside, twenty-seven pairs of hands played hand-clapping games. The sound bounced against the walls and ricocheted across the room from end to end. Hand-clapping led to singing, and singing to dancing.

I tried to join in, but whenever I approached a group, the girls would turn their backs to me. Some chirped through their teeth to show disdain or disgust. Others ran away, shouting, 'Devil child! Leopard girl! I don't want to catch your spots.'

Only Mabinty Suma would play with me. We were the outcasts, but I was going to change that, so I walked to the centre of the room. My father had always said I had 'an active imagination', and I was good at inventing stories and games. So I decided to win friends for Mabinty Suma and myself.

'I have a new indoor game,' I announced. All eyes turned to me, because in a world without any playthings other than a ragged ball, a new game is always welcome. 'This is a game that everyone must play. And I mean *everyone*,' I added, 'or it will not be much fun.' When I didn't hear hissing, I continued. 'To play the game, we must sit in a circle.'

I actually didn't have a game in mind in the first place and had to make one up on the spot. 'In this game we will tell the scariest story anyone has ever heard. One girl will start the story, and each girl after her will add to the story. The last girl in the circle will end the story.'

'What about the boys?' Omar, the tallest and brightest of the three boys, interrupted.

I rolled my eyes at him and chirped, but let them join us in the circle.

'I should be the one to begin this game,' bossy Omar announced.

'It is Mabinty Bangura's idea,' another girl named Kadiatu said. Omar began to protest, but he was out-numbered. 'You should begin,' Kadiatu told me, and so I did. 'In the jungle there is a half man, half leopard that eats children.'

Everyone screamed, and the next girl added a line to the story while we all shivered and giggled. By the end of the game I had made twenty-five more friends.

Chapter 6

A Victory

'Do you have another game for us?' Sento Dumbaya asked the following day as the rain drummed on the tin roof.

'Yes, I do,' I lied. Within minutes I invented another game, which involved singing and dancing as well as storytelling.

Every day of that rainy season, my heart leaped when someone asked, 'Do you have another game for us?' I could deal with the mean aunties and the small amount of rice if I had friends.

I refused to show that I was afraid of Auntie Fatmata, even though I really was, just like everyone else. When Auntie Fatmata raised her hand to strike my face, I didn't wince. When her switch whistled through the air and struck me, leaving welts, I didn't cry. The aunties loved to tug on our tightly braided cornrows, because it hurt so much but left no evidence of their abuse. This was important to them. Andrew Jah needed to send our pictures to America, so he did not want to see bruises on us.

When the aunties tugged on my cornrows, I squeezed my eyes closed. The pain took my breath away, but I wouldn't cry until I was out of sight of both aunties.

The more stoic I appeared, the more Auntie Fatmata tried to make me cry.

One night, when Mabinty Suma and I were sound asleep, Auntie Fatmata ground chilli peppers into a fine powder. Then, just before morning, she sprinkled it all over my face until it filled my nostrils, eyes and mouth.

I sat up and began to scream. My face felt like it was on fire. My eyes streamed with fiery tears.

I could hear Auntie Fatmata cackling. The louder I screamed, the happier she sounded. She had finally succeeded in making me cry. As Mabinty Suma dragged me stumbling to the wash bucket, I swore that I would get my revenge.

'We should tell Papa Andrew,' Mabinty Suma suggested. I smiled at my best friend. Despite our nearly identical names, we were very different. She turned to adults to solve her problems. I did not.

'If I tell Papa Andrew, he will yell at Auntie Fatmata. That will make it even worse. I have to fix this on my own.'

'But how?' she asked.

'I will find a way.'

~

While I was trying to find a way to get even with Auntie Fatmata, the mosquitoes hatched and most of us got malaria. Auntie Fatmata didn't torture us so much while we were sick with fever, vomiting and diarrhoea. But one night soon after I began to get better, Auntie Fatmata made one of the younger children go to the bathroom on my hair and face while I was asleep. I woke up gagging.

Mabinty Suma grabbed my hand and led me outside. I sobbed while she tried her best to clean our grass mat and me. Then it started to rain.

'Come in! Come in now!' Auntie Fatmata screamed, her voice drowned out by thunder as I stood outside, hoping that the lightning wouldn't strike me. I wondered if I might be better off if it did.

Suddenly a lightning bolt struck the ground beside us. Mabinty Suma jumped like a startled cat, but I stayed still. 'We could have been killed!' she shrieked.

'A lightning bolt won't kill me,' I bragged.

'And why not? Do you have voodoo powers?'

That was it! Mabinty Suma had given me the idea that I needed to fight off Auntie Fatmata. 'Yes,' I answered. 'I am a witch. Come, I'll show you!' I shouted into the rain as I grabbed her arm, and dragged her inside.

I had always been very flexible, and my skin stretched like soft rubber. I used to scare my cousins by flipping my eyelids inside out. Now I decided to put my 'talent' to work.

Auntie Fatmata stood inside with her flicking switch. I turned my eyelids inside out and rolled my eyeballs upward. I held my hands out in front of me and said in a deep voice, 'I am a witch. I will place a spell on you if you harm me.' The aunties were superstitious, and we lived in a place where many people practised voodoo, so I knew my trick would scare them.

With my eyes rolled into my head, I couldn't see the aunties, but later Mabinty Suma and the other girls told me that their eyes had bugged out and their mouths had hung open with shock. I didn't need to see them to know that I had frightened them badly, because they never again dared to lay a hand on me.

Chapter 7

The Gift of Harmattan

When the rainy season ended, we started school at the orphanage. Because I could read Arabic, I was placed in a class with older children. Together we began learning English and mathematics from Teacher Sarah. She lived nearby in Makeni and visited us every day. She was smart, kind, gentle and reminded me of my mother, so I worked hard to make her proud of me.

One day, after hearing Auntie Fatmata ridicule me for my spots, Teacher Sarah took me aside and said, 'Only the ignorant and superstitious will care about your spots. Papa Andrew is trying to send all of you to the United States of America. There you will be placed with a mama and papa who will not give a hoot about your spots. They will care only about your head.'

I reached a hand to my tight, thin braids. They had turned orange with malnutrition, and my hair was falling out. I must have looked doubtful about her words, because Teacher Sarah smiled and said to me, 'I mean that they will care about what is inside of your head . . . your intelligence . . . your ability to learn.'

After Teacher Sarah told me that, I worked even harder than before. I wanted to please my unknown American parents and my beloved teacher. And on the day that a red lorry arrived at the orphanage gates, I got my chance.

~

Usually the dry season brought the rice harvest, but this year, because of the debils, we were without food. When the driver of the lorry began unloading huge white bags at the gate, I sounded out the letters until I could read the red-and-blue print. 'Mealie meal super maize meal. Food!'

The aunties set about boiling the mealie meal in the rice pot. It didn't taste as good as rice or cassava, but it was healthier and filled our bellies.

'Who sent us this food?' I later asked Papa Andrew.

'Americans, the ones who are coming in March,' he answered.

Americans were coming in March! I had never seen an American. Nor had any of the other girls. We were so excited about the visit that we couldn't sleep that night.

'The Americans will be white,' Kadiatu announced from her mat across the room.

'White!' most of the girls exclaimed at once.

'What does a white person look like?' a girl named Yeabu asked.

'I've heard that they are the colour of our mealie meal, and you can see the sky through their eyes,' Kadiatu answered.

'Are they ghosts?' Mabinty Suma asked.

'No, they are human, like us, and they are all doctors or nurses. I know because my brother met some Americans,' Kadiatu informed us.

'Where?' I asked.

'At the hospital, when he had an operation on his face. My brother told me that the doctors wore green robes and masks over their faces,' she continued.

With my belly now full for the first time in a long time, I could think about something other than sickness and hunger. As I lay there in the dark, I thought about life in America, but despite Teacher Sarah's optimism, I worried that no American mother and father would want a spotted child.

I fell asleep, desperately missing my mama and papa. It was my birthday the next day, and I longed for them more than ever.

~

When I awoke the next morning, the air was thick with orange dust. I could not even see the sun, and the force of the Harmattan wind almost knocked me over. Auntie Fatmata told us to stay inside, but I was sure that I heard my father's voice carried by the wind. 'Come with me, Mabinty Suma,' I said to my friend. 'I want to walk to the gate to see if my father has come calling for me.'

'You are crazy, Mabinty Bangura. Your parents are dead, so how can your papa be at the gate?'

'But I never saw my papa's dead body, and I hear his voice,' I insisted.

'That is just the wind calling,' Mabinty Suma scoffed.

I shook my head. 'Maybe he didn't die. Maybe he is alive, and he has come to visit me for my birthday,' I declared as I tugged at her arm.

Mabinty Suma rolled her eyes and whined, 'If we go, Auntie Fatmata will be angry.'

'She won't beat me. She's afraid of me,' I reminded her.

'Ha! Well, she isn't afraid of me. *You* are the witch child, not me, Mabinty Bangura.'

What my friend said was true, so I patted her shoulder and said, 'You can stay here. I'm not afraid to go alone.' Then I pulled my T-shirt up over my nose and forced my way against the head wind. The particles of sand stung my skin like needles as I raced towards the gate.

I had run far when I heard Mabinty Suma coughing and calling my name. She was nearly invisible in the swirling clouds of dust. I retraced my steps to her, and hand in hand we headed for the gate.

We did not find my papa when we reached the gate. My heart sank as I watched long lines of strangers hurrying by. Men were pushing wheelbarrows filled with all their worldly goods. Women and girls with baskets of their belongings trailed behind them, babies in *lapas* clinging to their backs.

'Where are you going?' I called out to a girl about my age.

'The war has come to our town. We are running away from the debils. You should run away too,' she answered, and kept going.

I looked at Mabinty Suma and asked, 'Should we run away?'

'How can we do that?' she asked. 'We have no parents to protect us.'

I peered through the wrought-iron gate, hoping that someone would come to take me away. Just then I was slapped in the face. 'Ugh! Trash!' I exclaimed, but it wasn't trash at all. I had been attacked by the pages of a magazine. The magazine was stuck in the gate, exactly where my face had been. I reached my hand through and grabbed it.

It was filled with shiny pages printed with pictures of

white people. I squinted to look at it, though I was nearly blinded by the dust.

I grabbed Mabinty Suma, and together we ran to the shelter of a tree. 'Look! This is what white people look like,' I said as I held the fluttering magazine out to her.

'Why are they dressed so funny?' she asked, giggling as she held it inches away from her eyes.

I looked at the page she was pointing to. A white lady was wearing a very short, glittering pink skirt that stuck out all around her. She also wore pink shoes that looked like the silk fabric I had once seen in the marketplace, and she was standing on the very tips of her toes. 'Isn't that a funny way to walk?' Mabinty Suma asked.

'Hmm, I think that she might be dancing,' I said.

'Dancing! On tippy-toe? It's impossible to do that!' my friend exclaimed.

'Oh no. I think that I could do it, if I tried hard enough,' I said. Then I leaped to my feet and stood on the tips of my naked toes. I dropped back to the soles of my feet, and I twirled around, full of joy, despite the wind that stung my face and blew into my open mouth.

'Someday I will dance on my toes like this lady. I will be happy too!' I shouted into the wind.

At that moment we heard Auntie Fatmata screaming for us to come back. 'Hurry! Go. I'll follow you,' I said. Then I quickly ripped the picture out of the magazine as the wind tried to tear it from my hands, and folded it in half, and in half again. I stuffed it into my underwear, the one item of clothing that I owned. I ran back to the building with the magazine flapping in my hand.

When I saw how angry Auntie Fatmata was, I said, 'Look, Auntie Fatmata, I have a gift for you. It's a white person's magazine and it has many wonderful pictures.'

Ah, the look of confusion on her face was priceless. It must have been very difficult to allow the words *Thank you, Number Twenty-Seven* to spill from her lips.

Later I heard Auntie Fatmata complaining loudly to Auntie Sombo. 'Number Twenty-Six and Number Twenty-Seven were down by the gate in all of this wind. Stupid girls. Didn't they know that nothing good ever comes of the Harmattan?'

I grinned behind my hands. Then I stood on my toes and tried to twirl around the room, nearly tripping over the legs of the other girls. 'Ow! Oof! What are you doing, Mabinty Bangura? You are stepping on us,' Yeabu complained.

'I'm celebrating the Harmattan!' I exclaimed, giddy with excitement, knowing that some good does come from the Harmattan.

Chapter 8

White Ladies and Family Books

The following day, when we had finished our lessons with Teacher Sarah, I lagged behind as usual. 'Do you have to leave now?' I asked her as I did every afternoon while she gathered her belongings for the long walk home.

'Mabinty Bangura, what is on your mind?' Teacher Sarah asked.

'I found a treasure,' I answered as I carefully unfolded the picture I had kept hidden since the night before. 'I'm trying to read these words, but most are too difficult,' I said, and I held out the creased page.

'Oh, this is a picture of a ballerina,' she said, pointing to a word. 'This word, *ballerina*, is an Italian word. It means "little dancer". The woman in this picture is a ballet dancer.'

'What is ballet?' I asked.

'It is a kind of dance. It takes many years of practice to become good at it,' she explained as we walked towards the gate.

'Do you think that I could learn it?' I asked.

'Maybe . . . if you take ballet lessons,' Teacher Sarah answered.

'Could you give me ballet lessons?'

'Oh, I only wish that I had so much grace and talent,' she said. 'No, I cannot teach ballet, but I have a book about ballet at my parents' home in Freetown. The next time I visit, I'll bring it back for you,' she said, with a loving smile on her face.

I was so excited about the book that I ran hooting and hollering across the orphanage yard. Papa Andrew frowned at me.

'You are late, as usual. I am telling the other orphan pikins about the American ladies who will soon be visiting. Now sit down and be quiet.'

I hurriedly flopped into the space beside Mabinty Suma and listened as Papa Andrew warned us to be on our best behaviour. He frowned at me again when I raised my hand and asked, 'Are they bringing us back to America with them?'

'If you hadn't been late, Mabinty Bangura, you would have known the answer to that question. No, not now. They are coming to photograph you and examine each of you. They'll also immunise you,' he said.

I nodded my head knowingly. I knew what a photograph was, and I had been examined by a doctor once, an African doctor, but I didn't know what the word *immunise* meant. I raised my hand to ask Papa Andrew, but he ignored me. He had told me many times before that I asked too many questions for my own good. I decided to just wait and find out for myself what that long word meant.

~

The following morning we got up early to bathe and have our hair freshly braided. Papa Andrew lined us up at the gate by height, with the smallest first and the tallest last. He made us sing one of the English songs that Teacher Sarah had taught us as a car drove through the orphanage gate. We sang my favourite, '*Lapa, Lapa, Lapa* on My Shoulder', and eager to please, I sang at the top of my lungs.

My voice faltered when three ladies climbed out of the car. They were the strangest-looking women whom I had ever seen. They didn't look at all like the lovely ballerina in my magazine. These women had bright red faces and wild, frizzled hair. One had yellow hair. The second had orange hair, and the third had brown hair. They all had different-coloured eyes too.

'Ah yes. They are nurses, for sure. I can tell,' Kadiatu murmured with a voice of authority.

'I didn't know that white people came in different

colours, like Teacher Sarah's crayons,' I whispered into Mabinty Suma's ear.

The tallest woman said to us, 'I loved your singing! What language was it?' When Papa Andrew translated her compliment into Krio for us, we all giggled because we thought that we had sung in English.

Papa Andrew snapped his fingers and pointed at us one by one. We leaped to attention and helped the ladies carry boxes from their car to our classroom. When the boxes were unpacked, the ladies lined us up. The other girls hung back, but I pushed to the head of the line, tugging a nervous Mabinty Suma behind me.

One of the women smiled at me as she wrote my name on the first page of her notebook. Next, the second lady measured the thickness of my arm and my height. Then she weighed me. When she looked at the numbers on the scale, she pursed her lips and frowned. I began to worry. Maybe I didn't weigh enough to go to America.

The third lady squirted sweet juice into my mouth. It tasted pretty good, and I decided that if this were my immunisation, I wouldn't mind more.

Suddenly the second lady wrapped her arms tightly around me. I began to scream as the third lady grabbed my arm and was about to stab it with a needle. I wiggled and squirmed. I even tried to bite the woman who was holding me, but she didn't let me go.

The stab of the needle didn't last long, and I was rewarded with something called a lollipop. It was round, orange, and tasted even better than the sweet juice. Finally the third lady hugged me, patted me, and sent me out the door.

Once free, I strutted up and down the line of girls waiting for their turn. 'It's worth getting stabbed by a needle to get this round, sweet thing,' I explained as I held up the lollipop.

Mabinty Suma soon came out of the classroom sucking on a purple lollipop. I gave her a lick of mine, and she let me taste hers. The white American ladies gave us many more lollipops while they were here. They also painted our fingernails. During their visit, Papa Andrew fed us all kinds of treats, like chicken and okra. I was sorry to see the Americans leave, and I wished on a star that they wouldn't forget us.

~

My wishes came true. The American ladies didn't forget us. They sent us brushes for our teeth, barrels of clothes, shoes, screens for our windows, beds, long pipes that carried water from the well to the inside of our compound, and little packets of coloured powder called Kool-Aid.

Papa Andrew added the coloured powder to our

water when it tasted rancid. The Kool-Aid smelled like the lollipops, but it was bitter. It would be a long time before I told this story to someone in America and learned the reason why.... The Kool-Aid was supposed to be mixed with sugar, and sugar was expensive.

The best things that the Americans sent us were family books. Papa Andrew explained, 'These are books prepared by your new parents, and will be filled with pictures and messages from your new mamas and papas. Each of you will get your own book, except for sisters. They will share, because they will be going to the same family.'

From the day Papa Andrew mentioned the books until the day they arrived, we did nothing but imagine what our new American families would look like. I told everyone that my new mother would be young, tall and slim. She would dance on the tips of her toes. My father would be even taller. They would both be very smart and read a lot.

~

One night, when we were talking about our new families, Mabinty Suma fell silent. 'What's wrong? Why are you so quiet?' I asked her.

Then she burst into tears, saying, 'We are going to

have different mothers and different fathers. We might not even live in the same village.'

I gasped. That thought had not occurred to me. I had simply assumed that because we were best friends and our names were so similar, the same family would adopt both of us. Suddenly, getting adopted and moving to America didn't promise to be as much fun as I had thought it would be. Then the lorry arrived with the boxes of family books, and things got worse. Mabinty Suma and every other girl in the orphanage got a family book, but I did not. I felt a big empty space in my belly. It hurt worse than when I was hungry.

While all of the girls sat in a circle, laughing and sharing the pictures of their new families, I crept off and wandered to the classroom. Teacher Sarah was still there, cleaning. When she heard me enter the classroom, she looked up with surprise and said, 'Mabinty Bangura, why aren't you outside, sharing your family book?'

'I didn't get one,' I whispered. 'Nobody wanted me. I must be too ugly.' I burst into tears and ran to Teacher Sarah, who opened her arms wide and rocked me back and forth. 'Please,' I begged her. 'Adopt me. I won't eat too much, and I will help you take care of your new baby,' I said as I patted her growing belly. Teacher Sarah stayed with me for a long time that day, trying to comfort me.

Chapter 9

The Debils!

The debils had been wandering in and out of our town ever since the Harmattan. They bothered many of the people in town, but they left our orphanage alone. I had heard Papa Andrew tell the aunties and our night watchman that it was safe enough here during the day, but they should not go into the streets after dark, when the debils were drunk and crazy from drugs.

It was darker than usual when I walked Teacher Sarah to the gate that night. We heard the distant sounds of drunken laughter. 'Is it safe to walk home now?' I asked her.

'Yes, if I hurry,' she assured me.

I stood at the gate as I did most evenings when Teacher Sarah left. Tonight she moved faster than usual as she headed down the road towards her home. Suddenly, out of the darkness, two debil lorries drove by, lighting up the dirt road and catching Teacher Sarah in their headlights. They stopped, and laughing men and boys leaped to the ground.

'NO-O-O!' I shouted as they surrounded Teacher Sarah. I squeezed my skinny body through the wrought-iron bars of the gate and raced down the road towards her.

When I got there, several debils were holding her down by her wrists and ankles. A big debil, who was clearly the leader, stood there, shouting, 'Boy? Girl?' A large group of debils surrounded him, holding up fistfuls of paper money. The leader then raised his long, curved knife above his head.

When I saw what the debil was about to do, I threw myself on Teacher Sarah.

The debil leader laughed at me, picked me up by my shirt, and flung me aside as though I were no heavier than a bug. Then he slashed downward with his knife and cut into Teacher Sarah. Blood spurted everywhere, covering me from head to toe.

The debil reached inside of Teacher Sarah and pulled out her unborn baby. He examined it and shouted, 'A girl!' Several men groaned. They had bet that the baby was a boy, so they had lost their money. Others, who had gambled on a girl, shouted in triumph.

The debil leader laughed just as Teacher Sarah's undersize baby girl drew her first breath and opened her eyes. He then tossed the infant into the bush on the side of the road. I ran into the bush to try to save the baby. If I couldn't save my teacher, at least I might try to save her baby, but a young debil dragged me out kicking and screaming. He wasn't much older than me.

The debil leader then turned his attention to me. 'What do we have here? Are you causing trouble *again*?' He nodded to the child soldier. The little boy lunged for my chest with his knife, but when he looked into my eyes, he hesitated just long enough for me to take one step backwards. The knife grazed me only.

'Kill her, or I will kill you!' the debil leader screamed at the boy.

'Stop, please! Do not kill her, please. She is just a poor orphan pikin. What does it matter to you whether she is dead or alive?' a frantic voice begged. It was Uncle Sulaiman, the night watchman at the orphanage, who must have followed me out. I gasped when I saw him. Didn't he know that the debils wouldn't hesitate to cut off his limbs? However, the debil leader appeared to be amused by Uncle Sulaiman and asked, 'Why should I care?'

'You don't . . . you shouldn't. That's why it is just as easy for you to let her go,' Uncle Sulaiman said.

The debil leader nodded his head, as though considering his logic. 'Fine, take her. Just keep her out of my way,' he ordered.

Sulaiman tossed me over his shoulder and raced back to the orphanage. He brought me to the director, who beat me with a switch for leaving the orphanage.

In a strange way, I was almost grateful for the beating, because the sting of the welts took my mind away from the horror that I had witnessed. Papa, Mama and now Teacher Sarah . . . How could I go on? I wondered. Then I saw the tearful face of Mabinty Suma.

'Mabinty Bangura! Where were you? I was so worried. I thought you were dead!' she cried. I hugged her tightly, but I couldn't tell her what I had seen. That night I lay trembling, thinking of Teacher Sarah and unable to sleep.

~

The next morning Papa Andrew announced to us that Teacher Sarah would not be returning to teach us. The other children thought that it was the birth of her baby that kept her away. It would be many months before I could tell anyone what had happened.

The debils' attacks were getting worse and worse, and we began to feel unsafe, even behind our gate. A few days after Teacher Sarah was murdered, we all woke up to what sounded like a bomb exploding in the yard. All of us leaped to the window to see what happened. 'Debils! Hide!' I shouted when my eyes fell upon the camouflaged men who jumped from the green lorry that had crashed onto our property.

'Hide? Where?' Kadiatu cried out as she gazed about the room, eyes bugged out with panic.

'Under our new beds,' Mabinty Suma ordered.

We stayed under our beds for what seemed like for ever, though it probably was only a few minutes, before a booted foot kicked open the door. 'Tell your orphan pikins to come out,' a gruff voice ordered. 'I will not harm them.'

Then we heard Papa Andrew's voice assure us. 'Come out, pikins. You are safe.'

One by one, we came out from our hiding places. 'Hurry!' the debil leader barked as we scrambled to our feet. The sight that greeted us was horrifying. A tall man with grizzled hair was holding a gun to Papa Andrew's head. He was the same man who had attacked Teacher Sarah.

I gripped Mabinty Suma's ice-cold hand. If I was about to be killed, I wanted to die with someone I loved. I could see in the flickering light that several other children did the same. Sisters clung to sisters, friends to friends as we awaited our fate.

Much to my surprise the debils did not shoot us or chop off our limbs. Instead the leader ordered Papa Andrew to line us up and lead us out into the darkness of night.

'I hereby declare that this orphanage is now the headquarters of the Revolutionary United Front in

Makeni. I will spare your life, the lives of your staff, and the lives of your orphan pikins,' the debil leader said to Papa Andrew.

'Where will we live?' Papa Andrew asked.

'In the bush, where we members of the RUF usually make our beds,' the leader answered.

'May I get the children's adoption papers and passports from my office?' Papa Andrew asked.

Surprisingly the debil leader nodded his head and ordered his second-in-command to escort Papa Andrew to the office.

Mabinty Suma whispered in my ear, 'Mabinty Bangura, would you ask the debil man if we can get our family books?'

Without even thinking, I asked, 'May we get the books from our American families?'

The debil leader narrowed his eyes. Then he threw his head back and laughed. 'Pikin, you are once again trying my patience.' But, once Papa Andrew returned, the debil leader sent him off to get our family books.

As we got ready to leave, the debil leader warned, 'Do not think of escaping to the Guinea border. You will be killed for trying to leave Sierra Leone. Our country needs its people.'

I wondered why the debils were killing so many people if this was true, but it was better not to ask.

Papa Andrew, Auntie Fatmata, Auntie Sombo and Uncle Sulaiman herded us off the orphanage grounds. We left without anything except our family books and the papers that would enable most of us to go to America. We made our way through the jungle and over the mountains to the Guinea border. Yes, that's right. We were heading to the neighbouring country of Guinea, despite the threats of the debil leader.

I didn't have a family book to keep me going as we walked through the bush, so I pulled out the folded picture from the magazine. That picture was my only hope. It was my promise of a better life somewhere away from all this madness.

Chapter 10
Stepping Stones to America

We saw hundreds of dead bodies on our way out of Sierra Leone. The debils had taken machetes to many of them, but the majority of people, even small children, had been shot in the head. They lay sprawled on the ground with their eyes and mouths open in terror. I could tell how long they had been dead by the stink and the bugs that crawled over them.

At night we tossed and turned, hungry, afraid and driven nearly crazy with itching, because most of us had chickenpox. Mabinty Suma tried to comfort us all by singing songs from our days in the orphanage. My favourite was 'Let There Be Light', a song that she had made up. That song and the ballerina photo were the two things that reminded me that I was still alive.

~

One afternoon, when I felt that I could no longer put one foot in front of another, a voice boomed out of the dense bush. A man in uniform came out, startling us all. We made a beeline for the trees. Papa Andrew nearly dropped the child he was carrying in his effort to stop us. 'We are here! We are here! We have reached the Guinea border!' he shouted.

In my eyes one camouflage uniform looked like the other. The soldier at the border looked no different from the debils who had terrorised us, but we eventually came out from behind the trees. As we stepped into Guinea, a familiar face emerged from the crowd to greet us. It was Uncle Ali, the Sierra Leone agent of the American adoption agency. He was a mean man, and I wasn't usually pleased to see him, but my heart was happy to see him this time. I knew that he would get my fellow pikins from the border to their new homes in America. But where would I end up? The thought of being left made me feel like I had been stabbed.

~

Papa Andrew and Uncle Ali piled us into a lorry. We were taken to a makeshift village in which the huts were made out of thin plastic, making it look like a sprawling garbage-bag town. We were assigned to one of the huts, and we stood staring at each other in the heat as the sun poured down on our shelter. I was so hot, tired, hungry and sick that I was unsure of whether to cry in self-pity or laugh in celebration of our arrival.

The United Nations refugee camp in Guinea was not a place where we could laugh and play. The local trees, which had once stood tall, had been cut down to be the lodge poles upon which our plastic-bag huts were built. Trunks of the trees poked out of the ground, making it too dangerous for us to run around.

Before nightfall, a worker at the camp warned Papa Andrew that RUF rebels would try to sneak into the camp after dark. 'Keep the children inside,' he said. 'Any unaccompanied child is likely to be kidnapped or killed.' We sat huddled together on the ground inside the hut on that first night. In the morning Papa Andrew left us with Uncle Sulaiman and the aunties while he walked to the nearby town. Later that day, when the sun was at its highest and the inside of the plastic house was hot enough to bake us like cassava, he returned to collect us. 'I have made arrangements for us to move into a house in Conakry,' he said. 'You will be safer there. It is too far away from the border for the RUF to kidnap children.'

I had only known the Kenema District of Sierra Leone, where I was born, and the city of Makeni in the Bombali District. Conakry, Guinea, might have been halfway across the world, as far as I knew. 'Is Conakry close to America?' I asked.

'No, it is a stepping stone on the way to America,' Papa Andrew explained. 'The international airport is there. That is where we will board our flight out of Guinea to Ghana, and from there you will travel by plane again to America.'

My mouth dropped open, and I must have looked stunned, because Papa Andrew asked, 'How did you think you would get to America? Walk?'

'I thought we would ride in the back of a lorry,' I answered.

Papa Andrew laughed. It seemed that he often laughed when I said something. When I first met him, I thought that he laughed to make fun of me, so I would get mad. Now I knew that he laughed because he thought that I was funny, and I liked that.

'America is across the ocean,' he explained.

'Couldn't we ride in a boat?' I asked.

'That would take for ever, but what is your objection to flying in an airplane?'

'It might fall out of the sky, or I might feel sick up so high,' I answered, and he laughed once more.

'A ship might sink, and you would definitely feel sick on a ship,' Papa Andrew said. He was the only person in the plastic hut who seemed to find my words funny. Everyone else was too worried to laugh.

He was still shaking his head from side to side and chuckling to himself as he led us out of our plastic house to the road outside the camp. There, a wrinkled old man was waiting for us with a yellow-and-black taxicab. We had been in a lorry before, but none of us had ridden inside a car. We climbed into what we believed was the lap of luxury.

All of us pikins squeezed into the back of the taxicab. We sat on laps several children deep as the four adults in our party climbed into the front with the taxi driver. I couldn't see anything because I was buried somewhere under a pile of children. All I can remember from the ride was how sweaty it was and how much I felt like throwing up.

~

Our little house in Conakry wasn't much different from our orphanage in Makeni. We had no new beds in the Conakry house like the ones the Americans had sent to us in Makeni, so we made do with grass mats.

We also had no teacher and no books in Conakry either. Every day I thought of Teacher Sarah and the wonderful storybooks that she read to us, so my memories of her were both happy and sad.

Papa Andrew and Uncle Ali tried to buy books with the money sent to them by the American adoption agency so that we could continue our lessons, but there was none to be had . . . at least not books written in

English, because French is the official language of Guinea. So we pikins read our family books over and over again.

Of course, since I had no family book to read, I sat alone with a stick, writing words in the dirt.

'What are you doing?' Mabinty Suma asked.

'I am pretending that I have an American family, and this is my family book.'

'You don't have to pretend, Mabinty Bangura. I'll share my family book with you.'

'But that's your family, not mine,' I answered, with tears filling my eyes.

'Well, maybe when I meet my new mama, I can ask her if she wants two daughters,' Mabinty Suma said.

That cheered me up, so together Mabinty Suma and I read her family book. Together we recited the words: 'Hello, I am your American mother. Hello, I am your American father. You have three American brothers. Their names are Adam, Erik and Teddy. Teddy plays the piano.' Each time we read that, we'd ask each other, 'What is a piano? How do you play with it?'

Mabinty Suma and I would screech every time we came to the page that said, 'This is our family dog. His name is Alaska.' He was an enormous dog with long, sharp teeth and furry white hair. He was bigger than the two of us put together. 'Do you think he has rabies?' I'd ask, causing us to shriek louder.

'He looks like he wants to eat us!' Mabinty Suma would say, and again we'd scream.

The page I liked best was the one that said, 'This is our house at Thanksgiving. Thanksgiving is a holiday when we give thanks and eat turkey.'

'This turkey is the biggest chicken I've ever seen,' I'd comment. 'I can't wait to eat it.' Somehow I had convinced myself that this was my family as well as Mabinty Suma's. When I'd remember that the turkey didn't belong to my family because I didn't have a family, I'd feel that stabbing pain in my chest again and I'd start to cry.

Mabinty Suma preferred the page that said, 'This is your bedroom.' In the picture was a bright red bed with a colourful blanket. We could see dolls on the bed, and in the background were dresses hanging. I couldn't help feeling jealous that she'd soon be wearing those dresses, and I would be left behind with nothing but my rags.

Later on, she noticed that her bed had a top and a bottom. 'Look! My bed has two parts! There is enough room for you! I promise; I will ask my new mother if you can sleep on the top of my bed.'

Mabinty Suma and her bed with two parts gave me hope.

~

One day Papa Andrew called a meeting and announced, 'Tomorrow we are leaving for the airport. We are going to Ghana. It is another stepping stone to America. There you will meet your new parents.'

For a moment I forgot that I did not have a family. I joined the other children, hooting with joy, until Auntie Fatmata said to me, 'Number Twenty-Seven, what are you cheering for? Nobody wanted a spotted child. Papa Andrew told me that you were offered to twelve families, but all of them refused to have you. You are staying in Africa with me.'

The thought of staying behind with Auntie Fatmata filled me with terror. I jumped up and ran out of the room. Later Papa Andrew came looking for me. He explained to me that, at the last minute, a family had been found for me. I too would be adopted.

As excited as I was to have an American family, I had grown used to the idea that Mabinty Suma's family was mine too. I had lost everyone else I loved in the world. How was I going to live without my best friend?

Chapter 11

Into a Mother's Arms

Early the next morning we boarded the plane to Ghana. I was so nervous that I vomited all over my dress and Uncle Ali. The flight attendant brought wet paper towels and tried to wipe me clean, but even when the dress was clean, it still smelled awful.

When the plane landed, I was the first to see the white parents, but I could not stop to scrutinise them and guess which one belonged to me. Uncle Ali was angry with me for misbehaving on the flight from Guinea and for vomiting all over his pants. He hauled me past the crowd of onlookers, tugging my arm and walking so fast that my feet flew off the floor. He dragged me into the toilets and spanked me soundly before bringing me back past everyone a second time.

I was so embarrassed and angry that I couldn't stop scowling when I finally exited the gate with the other pikins. Mabinty Suma pinched my arm and said, 'If you wear such a grouchy face, the American families will not like you.' I ignored her, because I was suddenly distracted by the feet of the women.

I crouched down to examine their shoes, hoping that my mama would be wearing pink dancing shoes. Many of the parents were wearing sneakers. Sneakers were a luxury in Africa, and I desperately wanted a pair, though not quite as much as I wanted pink dancing shoes. The sneakers I saw were in dull colours like grey, tan, black or white. I did spy one pair of bright red sneakers that set one woman apart from the others. My gaze travelled from her feet to her face, and I recognised the mama in Mabinty Suma's family book. I grabbed Mabinty Suma's arm and tipped my nose in her new mother's direction.

The woman smiled at us. She came up to us and patted our backs. 'I'm your new mama,' she said to both of us. 'You're going to be sisters.'

Could this be true? I thought I understood the word *sisters*, but couldn't believe my ears. I squeezed Mabinty Suma's hand, and then I got so excited that I even pinched her arm. She must have been as happy as I was because she didn't get mad and pinch me back.

Finally our new mama took hold of our hands and led us away, and we knew that our dream of staying together was coming true. I thought that we would be taken directly to our new home in America – the one with the lake in the yard, the fierce white dog, the piano and the big Thanksgiving chicken, but we wouldn't be leaving to go to America for a while. We had entered Ghana without a visa and spent hours waiting for permission to enter that country.

I looked around at my friends. They sat with their new parents, looking scared and uncertain of what awaited them. I didn't feel scared. I had wanted to be Mabinty Suma's sister so badly that I felt sure I would be fine.

~

Mabinty Suma clung to our new mama as though she had known her for a lifetime. Suddenly Uncle Ali rose from his seat and ripped them apart. He said to Mama, 'You have enough to do with one child. I will hold this one.'

Mabinty Suma had always hated Uncle Ali, so it didn't surprise me when her chin quivered and the tears pooled in her eyes. Mama walked over to Uncle Ali and lifted Mabinty Suma from his lap. 'I've raised five sons,' she said. (Mabinty Suma and I would learn later that in addition to the sons we had already heard about, Adam, Erik and Teddy, our American parents had adopted two boys with haemophilia, Teddy's biological brothers, named Michael and Cubby, who died of AIDS before we arrived in the US.) 'I can certainly manage these two children.'

Uncle Ali's eyes blazed with fury. He wasn't used to

women standing up to him. When Mama returned to her seat with Mabinty Suma, I couldn't help but grin. I liked this new mother . . . very much.

~

After we finally received our visas, we were taken to be examined by doctors. They were African doctors who were paid by the American embassy to screen immigrants to the United States. The doctors took one look at my skin and spoke among themselves, wondering if my spots might be the result of a terrible disease called congenital syphilis.

Again my new mother stood up to these men. 'This child does not have congenital syphilis or syphilis of any kind. She has vitiligo.'

The doctors and I stared in wonder at Mama. She didn't look like anyone I'd ever seen, with pale yellow hair and eyes the colour of the sky.

'How do you know? Are you a doctor?' one of the African doctors asked her.

'Actually, I am a teacher of medical students,' she answered. The doctors immediately stopped arguing with her. They stamped a paper, and I was approved for entry into the United States.

With a mother like this, I knew I could do anything, even dance in pink shoes.

I didn't realise that my new mother was scared until I gripped her hand and felt that she was trembling. When we sat in the waiting area, she held me close to her. Before that moment I had remained aloof from her, but now everything had changed. She had defended me, protected me, just like my African mother would have done. She was my mother now, and I leaned back into her arms. It was a long time since I felt protected.

Soon it was Mabinty Suma's turn to be examined. With her bright eyes and dark, flawless skin, she easily earned the doctor's stamp of approval, though we later would learn that she had some serious medical problems.

When we returned to the waiting area, Mama wrapped her free arm around both of us, and we snuggled in close. We were sisters – part of a family now, with the good fortune to have found just the right mama.

~

Later that day we went to Mama's hotel. Mabinty Suma and I were thrilled to see that it had a real bed, just like the one that Papa Andrew used at the orphanage. We leaped onto the bed and bounced up and down in a fit of giggles.

Mama laughed and hauled us off the bed. She carried us still giggling into another room, where she flicked a little switch on the wall, and like magic, light flooded the space. Mabinty Suma and I tried flicking the switch too, and the lights went off. We pushed the switch up, and they turned on again. We pushed it down, and the lights turned off.

While we were entertaining ourselves with the light switch, Mama turned a knob in a white tub. Water splashed out of the pipe, which our mother called a faucet. She poured a capful of yellow liquid into the water, and bubbles began to fill the tub. Finally Mama helped us climb in. Our first bubble bath! Mabinty Suma and I were thrilled. 'Smell me!' I shouted with glee as I held up my hands. I had never smelled so good before.

When we were bathed, our mama wrapped us in towels, led us into the sleeping room, and presented each of us with clean, sweet-smelling clothes. Mine were pretty purple, and Mabinty Suma's were pink.

I had no sooner got dressed than I remembered! Off I dashed to find my beautiful ballerina picture from inside my old dirty clothes on the bathroom floor. Thankfully it was still there.

Mama began to unpack her luggage, pulling out some little dolls and bags of clothing. And then she found two pairs of sneakers that sparkled with pink glitter. When we stepped into them, lights flashed from our heels.

Even though I loved the glittery sneakers, I stood at my mother's side, patiently waiting for the one thing that I really wanted, while Mabinty Suma gathered up the beads and dolls and spread them over the bed to play. Mama looked down at me and said something. Though I didn't understand a word of her English, I could tell by the sound of her voice that she was asking me a question.

She unzipped all of the suitcases as though inviting me to search through them. Soon I was digging through piles of clothes and toys, checking all the nooks, crannies and zippered compartments of Mama's luggage. But Mama had not brought me pink dancing shoes. She crouched down in front of me and asked, 'What is it that you so desperately want, dear daughter?'

I tried to remember the English words that Teacher Sarah had taught me, but they wouldn't come to my lips. Instead I babbled on in Krio as I tried to explain about the ballerina and the special pink shoes.

My mother shook her head. Clearly she didn't understand me. Finally I pulled out my magazine picture and handed it to her. While she carefully unfolded it, I twirled around the room and stood on the tips of my naked toes.

My American mama gasped. Then she smiled and laughed. 'So you want to be a ballerina!' she exclaimed in a happy voice.

Ballerina! That was the word that Teacher Sarah had taught me. 'Yes,' I shyly answered.

My mama crouched down in front of me again and placed her hands on my shoulders. Very slowly she said, 'Home in America . . . you will dance.'

My heart beat rapidly in my chest. I became breathless with excitement. Mama understood me. She knew I wanted to dance. I was almost delirious with joy, knowing that my dream might someday come true.

Chapter 12

Michaela, Mia and The Nutcracker

On our second day in Ghana, Mama realised that every time she called, 'Mabinty', we both came running. Sharing the same first name hadn't mattered in the orphanage, where we were called by our numbers. But Mama didn't intend to call us Number Twenty-Six and Number Twenty-Seven. Instead she pointed at Mabinty Suma and said, 'Mia Mabinty.' She pointed at me and said, 'Michaela Mabinty.' Our African first names became our American middle names. One week later, when we boarded the plane to America, we were already answering to our American names.

~

I had a fever and slept for most of the long trip to the United States while Mia enjoyed looking out the plane's windows at the Sahara Desert, reading magazines and eating mounds of butter during our stopover in Germany.

My fever broke temporarily, and I awoke in time to land at the John F. Kennedy International Airport in New York City. From there we were driven south to our Cherry Hill, New Jersey, home in a shiny black car that was finer than any I had seen before. On the way, I was so hungry from not eating while conked out on the airplane that I begged for rice. The driver pulled over, and Mama took us inside a building that she called a rest stop, though no one seemed to be resting there.

I was overwhelmed by the amount of food in the rest stop. There wasn't any rice, but Mama bought us whatever we pointed to: hot dogs, fried chicken, orange juice and ice cream. Mia and I ate everything!

～

Eventually we pulled up in front of a beautiful blue house surrounded with tall trees. An older white-haired man and two dark-haired young men came out to greet us. Mia and I knew from our family book that they were our father and older brothers Teddy and Erik. I also remembered the page that said, 'Adam is your oldest brother. He is married and lives one hundred miles away.' So I was not surprised that Adam was not there.

I trusted my new papa immediately, but I was leery of the younger men. I wanted to ask if they were debils, but I was too afraid. I finally decided that, since they were not carrying knives or rifles and since my new mother hugged them, they probably were not debils.

We had held on to the backpacks Mama had given to us tightly the entire way home because they were the first things that we ever owned. Now, whether Teddy and Erik were brothers or not, we wouldn't let them touch our backpacks. We hoisted them onto our backs and followed Mama into the house.

In Africa women stick together, and men generally go about their own business. A girl's mother is always her greatest influence, friend and adviser. I suppose this is why, from that very first day in my new home, I felt a special bond with my new mother.

That first day, as I wandered through the house that belonged to my new family, I was ecstatic to discover the inground pool and begged to swim. Mia was less impressed with the pool than she was by the piano in the living room. We both remembered the picture of Teddy playing the piano. Now, as Mia stood across the living room staring at the strange object, Teddy sat down on a bench and began playing it.

When he touched the white and black keys on the piano, music wafted out of the instrument, and Mia's face lit with joy. In Africa she and I had thought that this large object was a toy, because Mama had written on the photo, 'Teddy, playing the piano.' We didn't have any idea that a piano made music. After that first day Mia and I often fought over whose turn it was to play the piano.

~

Because Mia and I had both arrived in the United States sick, we spent a lot of time in the doctor's office, where we were stuck with needles many times. The antibiotics that the doctor prescribed for me healed the terrible case of tonsillitis I had arrived with. The doctor told my mother that if I had remained in Africa another day or two, the infection would have spread through my body, causing sepsis. I surely would have died.

With the exception of the needles, my new world was a wondrous one. The first time I went to the supermarket, I couldn't believe the amount of food that lined the shelves. At first I was reluctant to touch any of it, but then I saw my mama and papa picking up fruits and piling them into a cart, and I joined in. Mia joined me, and together we grabbed at everything in sight. We began running up and down the aisle, filling our arms and our mouths as our parents chased us.

Suddenly Papa grabbed me and tossed me into the front seat of one of the carts. Mama did the same to Mia. I began to cry with frustration until Mama handed me a red box and popped a tiny, wrinkled brown fruit into my mouth. It was sweet and utterly delicious.

It didn't take me long to devour the entire box of raisins.

After Mama and Papa had each filled a cart with food, they stood in a line and gave a woman their small plastic card. I was amazed that we had been given all of this food for free! I wanted one of those plastic cards for myself. That night in bed Mia and I tried to think of ways to make our own plastic cards.

A few days later Mama took us to another even more enormous building. She called it a mall. It was like the bazaar in Makeni; only it was indoors, cleaner, and better. This time, instead of food, we bought clothes.

I wanted everything that I saw. I ran over to a purple dress and tried to pull it down off its hanger. When Mama said, 'No!' I went crazy. All she would have to do was swipe her plastic card, and the dress would be mine. 'Why! Why!' I shouted.

Mia started grabbing at dresses too. Mama had to pick us up and carry us kicking and screaming out of the shop. It took quite a few trips to the mall before Mia and I learned that we couldn't have everything that we wanted.

~

Life in America was fun, with new adventures every day. In the late summer Papa drove us to the seashore.

There, he lifted us high as breaking waves threatened to knock us down. He dug a deep hole in the sand and collected seashells with us. As we strolled along the beach, Mama pointed across the water and said, 'I first met you there, on the other side of the ocean in Africa.' I looked in fascination. I was glad that I was now on this side of the ocean.

When the sun set, we walked on the boardwalk, where we ate pizza and climbed onto the rides. We rode helicopters, fire engines, a Ferris wheel and horses that went up and down in the carousel. I remember how high those wooden horses seemed. At first Papa would stand by my side to keep me safe. I think it was while on that carousel that I knew I once more had a father to protect me.

~

Towards the end of the summer Mama took us to a farmers' market to buy fabric to make new curtains for our bedroom. Papa had given each of us two dollars to spend however we chose. We passed a stall that sold movies.

'Let's see what they have here. Hmm, how would you girls like to pick a movie to watch at home?' Mama asked as she browsed through the piles of videos that cost only ninety-nine cents each.

Suddenly my eyes lit up. 'Mama, look! I think this is a ballet movie,' I said in my heavily accented English. I no longer spoke Krio, not even to my sister, because Mama had promised to sign me up for ballet lessons as soon as I could understand and speak English.

Mama took the box from my hand to examine it. 'Michaela, what a clever little girl you are! This is the Balanchine *Nutcracker*, performed by the New York City Ballet!'

She handed it back to me, and I twirled around on my toes. I was happy to have this ballet movie, especially because we had lost a piece of luggage on our return trip from Africa. I no longer had the picture of the ballerina, which had been such an important part of my life in Africa. I proudly handed one of my dollar bills to the cashier to pay for *The Nutcracker*.

Later that day, while Mama sewed the new curtains for our bedroom, Mia and I watched *The Nutcracker* over and over again. I took it to bed with me that night and played it again the next morning and every day afterwards. Mia and I would dance along to it in our family room.

What I had only been able to imagine when I first looked at the magazine picture of the ballerina had now become reality. Soon I was begging for those ballet lessons that Mama had promised me in the hotel room in Ghana. Mama hung a calendar on the wall of our bedroom and circled the date 13 September 1999. Then she wrote, *Ballet Lessons*, in red ink, and I was over the moon with joy.

Chapter 13
Baby Emma

From morning until bedtime, my new life as Michaela was totally different from my life as Mabinty. I awoke in a soft bed, snuggled under a cosy duvet with a rainbow on it. Then I would hurry downstairs to the bright, cheerful kitchen, where my mother, who would be reading at the kitchen table, would greet me with a smile and a warm hug.

I loved opening the kitchen cabinet to choose my cereal for breakfast. I would pour it into a bright yellow bowl and add a scoop of fruit, either strawberries, blueberries or raspberries. Then I'd pour in a cup of milk. Having so many choices made me feel giddy with joy.

Best of all, I could eat until my belly was full. I didn't have to wait until someone filled the bowls for twenty-six other children.

When I needed to use the toilet, I could just jump up and run to the bathroom. I didn't have to worry about someone stealing my food if I left it behind. I flushed without fear of falling into a pit of smelly waste. Then I washed my hands with a foamy pink soap that squirted from a bottle. Ah yes, in America everything smelled good, I thought, even the toilet!

There were lights everywhere in my new home. At first Mia and I would run around, flicking them on and off. There were so many switches to so many things, like the machines that churned and whined all over the house. There were big, noisy machines for cleaning. One machine washed the clothes, a second machine dried the clothes, and a third machine washed the dishes. There was even a machine for sucking the crumbs and dirt from the floors.

Mama didn't have to light the wood fire to cook rice. In my new house she cooked on a stove with a hot top, but no flames. 'Where is the fire?' I asked the first time I watched her cook.

'It runs by electricity,' Mama explained as she slid a pan of cookies into the oven. I flicked on the light in the oven to watch in wonderment as the cookies gradually turned crispy and golden.

After breakfast Mia and I would choose something to wear. Mia and I had a closet full of colourful dresses to choose from. We would giggle and chatter away as we debated whether to wear pink, purple, polka dots or print. We always chose matching outfits, and people often thought we were twins.

Our parents encouraged us to try a different kind of

food every day, so that we could get used to eating new foods. In Sierra Leone all that we had ever eaten were rice, pepper, mealie meal, cassava, mango and banana. Now Mama and Papa wanted us to taste corn, peas, carrots, applesauce and many other strange foods. Mia and I liked 'tinky-winks' best. Everyone else called them buffalo wings, but that was such a long name to learn. After a while even the waitresses in the nearby diner ended up calling them tinky-winks, and they called us their favourite girls.

~

In America, no one teased me and no one abused me. Unlike Auntie Fatmata, my new mama and papa didn't use a switch to punish me. Instead they used a time-out chair, where I would be forced to sit still and be quiet for three minutes when I couldn't behave.

Mama made a rules sign to help us learn better behaviour. She hung it on the door. Several times a day she would say, 'Let's read our rules.' We were so excited about reading English that we gladly read the rules aloud:

Rules
1. No hit.
2. No bite.

3. No pinch.
4. No scratch.
5. No say caca.

Soon we were no longer hitting, biting, pinching, scratching or using potty language. The only things we continued to abuse were our baby dolls. We would beat them and shout at them, shaking them until their heads nearly fell off, mimicking the way Auntie Fatmata treated the children in the orphanage.

~

We had been with our new family for two months when, one day, our adoption social worker called Mama with a problem. She had a birth mother who wasn't sure whether or not she wanted to keep her baby or put her up for adoption, and she needed a week or so to make the decision. The social worker wondered if Mama and Papa would be willing to care for the newborn baby for a week. Mama said yes, and Baby Emma came to live with us for a short while.

Mama would wheel Baby Emma's pram from room to room so that she'd never be alone. She would pick up Emma and rock her in the rocking chair. Mia and I would sit on the floor in front of her, holding our dolls as we watched her care for the tiny infant.

She would say to us, 'A good mama hugs her baby gently. A good mama doesn't hit her baby. A good mama says nice words to her baby and rubs her back. A good mama kisses her baby and lets her know she is loved.' By the end of the week Mia and I knew that Auntie Fatmata's way was not the right way to care for babies.

On the day that the social worker picked up Baby Emma to bring her home to her birth mother, Mama let us each hold her for a few minutes. She took pictures of us with her. In my picture I am kissing Baby Emma's head so that she would know she was loved.

~

Our mama and papa took us on a holiday to Vermont the day after Baby Emma left so that we wouldn't miss her too much. But we missed her anyway and talked about her the whole trip. Two months later Santa Claus brought us each a doll that looked exactly like Baby Emma. We each named our new dolls Baby Emma, and practised taking good care of our babies, just like Mama had taken care of the real Baby Emma. Between our list of rules and Baby Emma's visit, Mia and I learned to become gentle in our play. Neither of us ever struck each other or another child after that.

Chapter 14

Into the World of Ballet

Though no one made fun of my spots in America, sometimes a child would point at me and ask his parent, 'What's wrong with that little girl?' Then I would want to crawl into a hole and disappear. If we were far enough away from the child, we just walked away as though we didn't hear him. Sometimes we were standing so close that we couldn't ignore him. Then Mama would explain vitiligo, and eventually I learned to do that too because Mama said, 'Sometimes it's better to answer the child's question so that he'll understand there's nothing at all wrong with you. Sometimes kids are just being curious, not mean.'

~

When it came time for my first ballet lesson, I dreaded wearing a leotard. We had visited the dance studio on the day that Mama registered Mia and me. There I discovered that we would be facing a mirror the entire time. I hated the idea of staring at my spots in the mirror through an entire lesson, so when we went shopping for dance wear, I insisted on a poloneck, long-sleeved leotard.

Mia and I tried on our new leotards, tights and ballet slippers the second we arrived home. I turned on *The Nutcracker* videotape, and we danced for hours in the family room. I was squirming, scratching and dripping with sweat while we danced, but Mia was comfortable in her cap-sleeved leotard.

That evening over dinner, Mia told our father all about our dance-wear purchases. I sat sulking while she went on to describe her new pink leotard.

'Michaela, what's wrong?' Papa asked.

'My leotard is hot. It makes me itch,' I complained.

'Does your leotard make you itch too?' he asked Mia.

'Of course not. Mine has short sleeves and a neck like this,' she answered, drawing a U on her chest.

'Is your leotard different?' Papa asked me.

Tears pooled in my eyes, and I said, 'Yes, mine has long sleeves and a poloneck.'

'Why did Mama choose a different leotard for you?'

'She didn't choose it. I did. I chose it so that I couldn't see my spots in the mirror,' I answered, feeling very much like Number Twenty-Seven again as I swiped at the tears that now dripped down my cheeks.

'Oh, sweetie, you won't need to wear that hot

leotard,' Mama said. 'I bought a second one just like Mia's, in case you changed your mind.'

'But the kids will see my spots, and I'll see them in the mirror,' I said, feeling sorry for myself.

Mama wasn't into self-pity. She said to me, 'Well, sweetie, you won't be able to wear a long-sleeved leotard with a poloneck when you're a world-famous ballerina, so you might as well get used to not wearing one now.'

Though I was usually stubborn, for once I took her advice without argument. The next day I went off to ballet class wearing the pink cap-sleeved leotard with the low neckline.

~

When I walked into dance class with Mia and ten other little girls, my expectations were high. I had already memorised the choreography of the Balanchine *Nutcracker*, so I expected to come out of class dancing like a real ballerina. Much to my disappointment, only one half of the session was ballet, and the other half was tap. I had nothing against tap, but I wanted the whole session to be ballet.

We learned our five basic positions, and how to plié and tendu. I expected us to immediately move on to greater things, like arabesques, grands jetés and pirouettes, but we couldn't. Two of the little girls cried for their parents, and the teachers took time to calm them down. Then some of the girls couldn't seem to get the dance steps quite right. Too soon the ballet half of class was done, and we were instructed to put on our tap shoes. Once the teachers finished tying the ribbons on our tap shoes, class was almost over.

When we came out of our lesson, Mia cheerfully skipped over to our mother and said, 'Mama, I just loved dance class!'

Mama took one look at my stormy face and didn't say a word to me until we got to the car. Then she asked, 'What's wrong, Michaela?'

'I hated it. They didn't teach enough ballet. I wanted to pirouette.'

Mama explained that dancing ballet was like reading a book. 'First you learn the letters. Then you learn the words. Finally you put the words together to make a story. You need to learn the simple steps, like tendu, before you can dance a full ballet.

'Let's give it another week or so, and see if it improves. If you don't like it any better, I'll find you a different dance class,' she promised.

That afternoon Mia and I showed Mama what we had learned. Then we ran off and watched *The Nutcracker*. First we danced the party scene, and then we danced 'Waltz of the Flowers'.

'Now *this* is what I mean by dancing,' I said as I danced the role of Dewdrop, tippy-toeing around Mia and the dolls I had arranged on the floor as flowers.

The following week I went to dance class thinking that we would progress to real dancing. We went over the same steps that we learned before. Before we could learn a new step, it was time for tap. By the third class I had learned to tell time. Now I noticed that we spent only twenty minutes on ballet and forty minutes on tap.

I stuck with that class for several more weeks, but the time we spent on ballet grew shorter as the time we spent on tap grew longer. 'Mama, I'm learning too much tap. I'm afraid I'll never learn to be a ballerina here,' I whispered into my mother's ear one afternoon after class.

~

At Christmastime Papa bought us tickets to see the nearby Pennsylvania Ballet Company dance *The Nutcracker*. Mama had sewn red velvet dresses with white eyelet pinafores for Mia and me. We wore those dresses with green ribbons in our hair and black patent-leather dress shoes on our feet. We looked like the Party Children in *The Nutcracker*.

When we entered the lobby of the Academy of Music

in Philadelphia, my heart skipped a beat; the Sugar Plum Fairy was seated there, and children were lined up to have their pictures taken with her. Mia and I lined up too, and I decided at that moment that I would one day dance the role of the Sugar Plum Fairy.

The performance was breathtaking. I sat spellbound, watching every step and every movement of the dancers' arms and heads. After the ballet Papa said, 'What did you think about that, girls?'

I said, 'It was nearly perfect!'

'Nearly? Why nearly?' he asked.

'Because in the snow scene, one of the dancers raised the wrong arm and stepped on the wrong foot,' I answered. 'I'd like to see it tomorrow again. Maybe then it will be perfect.'

My parents laughed. 'Just one *Nutcracker* a year,' Papa said.

'But we'll see a different ballet later in the season,' Mama promised.

Over dinner Mama asked, 'What role would you like to dance, if you could?'

'Soon I'd like to dance the role of a Party Girl or Marie, but when I get bigger, I want to dance the Arabian and the Sugar Plum Fairy,' I answered.

'What about you, Mia? What was your favourite part?' Papa asked.

'I liked the orchestra best,' my sister answered. 'I

liked that black instrument with the silver keys and the pointy top. That one played a note, and everybody else followed. What was it?'

'The oboe? You watched the oboist the entire time?' Mama asked.

'Not the entire time. I watched the dancers some of the time, but I always listened for that instrument with the pointy top . . . the oboe,' Mia explained.

That night Mia and I talked about *The Nutcracker* until late into the night. We were so excited that we had difficulty sleeping. When I finally did, I dreamt of dancing on the stage at the Academy of Music.

~

Just days before my fifth birthday, my mother took me to Philadelphia to register me for ballet lessons at the Rock School for Dance Education. Mia came with us, but she didn't sign up for class. 'I like tap dancing. I don't want to change dance schools.'

When I was introduced to the director of the school, I raised my leg straight up into the air and held it there. 'See what I can do? I want to learn to do even more,' I said. The director laughed and put me into Pre-Ballet II.

My new dance class at the Rock School was so much more fun than the class I had been taking. My teacher made it interesting. He taught us real ballet steps and let us make up our own combinations. Best of all, we didn't have to stop to put on tap shoes.

At the end of the term the Rock School would be performing a showcase at the Academy of Music, the same place where I had seen *The Nutcracker*. We were rehearsing for the showcase when our ballet teacher had us join hands to form a circle. As I reached out to link my hand with the girl beside me, she pressed her hand to her mouth and looked at me with horror. She then whispered to the girl beside her and pointed to my neck and chest.

I felt like Number Twenty-Seven all over again. I looked across the room at my reflection in the mirror. *You are one ugly girl,* I told myself, but at that very moment, Nora, the oldest and best dancer in the class crossed the room towards me. Then, raising her hand, she said to the teacher, 'May I dance next to Michaela? She's my best friend.'

Nora stood beside me and squeezed my hand, whispering, 'You're a good dancer for such a little kid.' I was thrilled. Nora was the one who was good. She had been dancing ballet for three years, and I admired her. I just could not believe that she would single me out for attention. For the rest of the year I stood directly behind her in class and mimicked every movement that she made.

The day of the showcase finally arrived. As Mama walked me into the Academy of Music, I tugged at her hand. She leaned over, and I whispered into her ear. 'Please notice if you can see my spots from the audience. If you can't, then I know that I can be a professional ballerina someday.' But when I walked onto the stage, all of my worries flew from my mind. I was just thrilled to be dancing on such a grand stage.

When the audience applauded, I felt a rush. It was such an intoxicating feeling that I knew I could not live without it. I realised then that I just had to become a professional ballerina.

During intermission I threw myself into Mama's arms and asked, 'Well, did you see them?'

'No . . . not at all,' Mama whispered, like a conspirator. 'It was like magic. From a distance they looked like a sprinkling of pixie dust or glitter.'

I sighed and said, 'Now I know that I will be a professional ballerina.'

It took me years to realise that my mother had lied to me that evening, but it was a good lie. At that point in my life, I needed to believe that my hated spots looked like magical pixie dust and would not stand in the way of my dream.

Chapter 15
A New Sister

Our childhood in Africa had been different from that of most American kids, so it took me and Mia a while to get used to playing with them. I thought it was very funny when snack time rolled around and one of my kindergarten friends exclaimed, 'Finally! I'm starving!' I looked at all the plump arms and legs, and knew that no one in my class was starving.

One day during recess the boys were playing with sticks and pretending that they were guns. Eddie, the biggest kid in our class, shot at Todd and said, 'Bang, bang! You're dead.'

Todd fell to the ground, folded his hands neatly on his chest, and closed his eyes.

'Look, Todd's dead,' Eddie said.

I walked over to Todd and looked down at him. I rolled my eyes. 'Todd's not dead,' I scoffed.

'Yes, he is,' Eddie argued.

'Mia, come here and look. Is Todd dead?' I asked.

Mia looked down at Todd and giggled. 'Of course Todd's not dead.'

By now all of the other kids gathered around us to listen to our argument. 'How do you know that Todd's not dead?' one of the girls asked me.

'Because I've seen a lot of dead people, and that's not what a dead person looks like.'

'Well, what does a dead person look like?' Eddie asked.

'I'll show you,' I answered. I lay down on the ground, opened my eyes wide, and let my mouth fall open. 'That's exactly what a dead person looks like,' Mia confirmed as she looked down at me. Both she and I gained a certain degree of respect from our peers because we knew what dead people looked like.

~

The following year I started to take ballet and other types of dance at a school closer to my home in New Jersey. Though I had a passion for ballet, I now found that I loved all kinds of dancing. Mia and I had a great time taking jazz and tap together. Yet no matter how much fun I had in those classes, ballet was my first love. I couldn't live without it.

Suzanne Slenn, my ballet teacher, said, 'You were fortunate to have been born with naturally great extension and talent. I expect more of you because of that.' So I worked very hard to please her.

I didn't have such good control of my extension in those days. While other children were having their parents or their dentists pull out their baby teeth, I was knocking mine out with my feet when I did grands battements.

One afternoon, when my mother was at the supermarket next door to the dance school, I ran out of ballet class with blood pouring out of my mouth. My friend Samantha's mother helped me wash the blood off my face and leotard. She comforted me by telling me that I had kicks so high that even a Rockette would envy them.

~

Right around the time my teeth were coming out, two other important things happened to me . . . and to my family. We got a new sister, and we began homeschooling.

One afternoon we got a call out of the blue from the adopted mother of Isatu Bangura, another girl from our orphanage. Isatu had been called Number Two by the aunties because they loved her. Mia and I loved her too and stayed in touch with her in America, but Isatu's adoption wasn't working out.

When the telephone rang, we were sitting at the kitchen table planning a trip to Scotland to celebrate my parents' wedding anniversary. My mother excused herself from our planning to take the phone call upstairs.

About half an hour later, Mama came down and asked Papa, 'Can we take Isatu?'

Papa said, 'Of course not!'

Mama looked stunned. 'But why not?' she asked.

'Isatu's not our child. Do you know how complicated it would be to take someone else's child to a foreign country?' my father asked.

'Oh, please, please . . . can Isatu come to Scotland too?' Mia and I chimed in.

'Oh, I don't mean to take her to Scotland,' Mama said. 'I mean, can we adopt her? Her American mother isn't able to keep her, and I'd hate to see her have to go into foster care.'

Papa laughed. 'I thought you wanted to take her to Scotland with us. Of course we can adopt her!' That's my father. He always sweats the small stuff, like what kind of cereal to buy at the supermarket, but when it comes to the big, momentous decisions like adoption, he responds immediately with an open and generous heart. Mia and I were so happy. We hugged our parents and planned for our new sister to arrive.

~

On Isatu's first night with us, I lay awake thinking about how strange fate is. Here Mia and I were, Number Twenty-Six and Number Twenty-Seven, the two least favoured children from the orphanage, and we were now beloved by our mama and papa. Isatu, on the other hand, had been a favourite of the aunties as Number Two, but her situation was reversed when she arrived in America. I could make no sense of this, but felt immensely thankful for where fate had landed me.

~

Soon after Isatu arrived, she said, 'It's not fair. Mia and Michaela are *M* names, but I have an *I* name.' I suggested that she change her name to something more exotic, like Svetlana, Tatiana or Natalia, names of Russia's most famous ballerinas. But Isatu said, 'No, I want an *M* name.' So she became Mariel.

~

We began home-schooling when Papa started working for a Japanese company. His work hours changed so that they would overlap with the working day in Japan. This meant that he left for work later in the morning, but he came home much later at night. Mia, Mariel and

I missed spending time with our papa. He used to read to us every night, but now we saw him only in the mornings and on weekends.

One night I missed Papa so much that I lay awake until I heard him come home. Then I tiptoed down the stairs and threw myself into his arms. 'Papa! I miss you!' I cried out.

'I miss you too,' he said as he held me in a bear hug. He said to Mama, 'I adopted these three little girls, but I hardly ever get a chance to see my princesses.'

The next morning Mama said, 'Would you girls like to be home-schooled? Then you can wake up later and have breakfast with Papa. At night you can eat dinner late with Papa, and he can read you bedtime stories again.' Because Mia, Mariel and I were best friends as well as sisters, we liked the idea of having our own home-school, so we happily said, 'Yes!'

I'm glad that we agreed, because home-school turned out to be fun. We were able to get all of our schoolwork done early enough to have our lessons and team practices on time. Best of all, we spent time with Papa when we got home.

~

Home-schooling also made it easier for me when I returned to the Rock School at the age of seven. I never had to worry about going to sleep late or waking up early in the mornings.

Because I was a little older and more experienced this time, I had to audition to see what level I'd be in that autumn. I was hoping to get into Level 1 or possibly into Level 1X. I was totally shocked and thrilled when I was accepted into the Level 2 ballet class . . . the first pointe class.

I felt little pitter-patters in my heart the day I tried on my first pointe shoes. The satin felt exactly like I had thought it would when I found the photo of the ballerina in the magazine. As I held the barre in the pointe-shoe store, I rolled up onto the tips of my toes, like my teacher had taught us. Suddenly I felt taller and more elegant. I removed my hand from the barre and balanced en pointe for the first time in my life. I felt so happy that I almost cried! I couldn't believe that, the very next day, I would dance in class en pointe. That night I rubbed the satin of my new pointe shoes with my fingers as I fell asleep, dreaming of becoming a real ballerina.

Chapter 16
The Canned-Food Birthday

Mia, Mariel and I were the same age. With our short haircuts, long legs and deep chocolate skin, we passed for triplets. Though this was fun for us, it sometimes created a lot of confusion. When we joined the swim team at our community centre, our names were usually listed on the meet sheets by first initial, last name, so we were each M. DePrince. At meets, each swimmer was only allowed to swim three events. At one meet I overheard a boy from another team complaining to his mother, 'It just isn't fair! Why can I only swim three times? I've seen M. DePrince swim nine times!'

We were a busy threesome. Besides going to swim team practice, we took dance and music lessons. Though we swam on the same team, we were always in different dance classes and we played different musical instruments. We never felt lonely being home-schooled, because we had each other and friends from our swim team and dance classes.

One night, shortly before my eighth birthday, I

watched the news on television with my brother Teddy and learned that the local food shelf was running out of food.

'What's a food shelf?' I asked Teddy.

'It's a place that people go to get free food, if they've run out of money.'

I had never before thought that people might be hungry in America. This shocked me. I asked, 'What kind of food does the food shelf need?'

'Oh, I suppose it needs canned goods, like peas, corn, beans, carrots, spaghetti. . . . Why, Monkey, are you planning to donate canned goods?'

I wrapped my arms around Teddy's neck and asked, 'If I do that, will you help me?'

'Sure, you know I would,' he answered.

The next afternoon, when my mother, my sisters and I were baking holiday cookies, I asked, 'Mama, can I have a birthday party?'

'Of course, sweetie,' she answered. After she slid the cookie sheets into the oven, she washed her hands, grabbed a pen and a pad of paper from a kitchen drawer, and sat down at the table with me. 'Who do you want to invite?' she asked.

'Jamie, Tabrea, Sabrina, Lauren, Briana, Katie, Annie, Rachel, Maria, Adriana, Jessica, Kaitlyn, Kristin . . .' On and on I went until I had over thirty-five girls on the list. 'Wow! That's a lot of girls! What kind of a party were you thinking of having?' Mama asked me.

'Oh, I would love to have a real ball and wear a gown like Sleeping Beauty or Cinderella.'

'What if the girls you're inviting don't own gowns?' she asked me.

'They can just wear a special dress, or they can borrow dresses from each other.'

'Just think of all the gifts you'll get,' Mariel said as she kneaded cookie dough at the kitchen counter, occasionally popping some raw dough into her mouth.

'Don't eat the raw dough!' I snapped, because I was irritated that she was adding her two cents to my party plans. 'I don't want them to buy me a gift. All I want for my birthday are cans,' I said.

'Cans?' my mother asked.

'Cans?' Mariel repeated.

'Cans, like cans of food?' Mia asked.

'Yep, cans . . . like cans of peas, cans of corn, cans of fruit. I want to donate cans to the food shelf. I heard on television that the food shelves that give food to the poor are running out of cans.'

Mama liked my idea, but told me that she'd have to look into it. The next week she discovered that it cost only seventy-five dollars to rent a hall in a local hotel. 'And the birthday cake comes with that price!' she exclaimed.

When Teddy came over for dinner, I reminded him that he had promised to help me collect cans for the food shelf.

'Okay, I'll help. Just tell me what you want me to do,' he said.

Teddy was a DJ, so I asked if he would DJ my party. He agreed, so on my birthday he and his girlfriend played music and taught all of my friends the hokey-pokey, the electric slide, cotton-eyed Joe, and other fun dances. Teddy's hair was dyed blue that night. My friends all thought that he was cute and supercool. That made me feel so proud of him. It was like having a celebrity for a big brother.

I wore a burgundy A-line gown with gold sparkles on the top. Papa said that I looked beautiful, and my sisters and friends looked beautiful in their dresses too. We all felt like we were Hollywood stars going to the Academy Awards. The *Philadelphia Inquirer* even sent a reporter and photographer to cover the event, just like it was a big social affair.

That night, after the party, Adam helped Mia and me weigh each bag of groceries on our scale. After I added the pounds, I learned that I had received 1,824 pounds of canned goods for my birthday. That was nearly a ton of food! Adam and my mama helped us carry all of the groceries to a food shelf in Camden, New Jersey. As we talked to the woman in charge of the food shelf and she told us about the many families that would use our canned food, I realised that giving something on my birthday felt a lot better than getting gifts. It was a feeling that I've never forgotten.

Chapter 17
Fears

Life was good for me in America. I had pretty clothes, plenty to eat, and lots of love. My family took fun holidays to the beach, Arizona and even to Walt Disney World. Best of all, I danced. I would have liked to leave all of my bad memories and heartbreak behind in Sierra Leone, but I didn't. I had frequent nightmares. In one dream my African mama was being chased by debils and struggled to escape them, but she was held back by me. I was too small to run fast. When the debils caught us, I'd wake up panicked and sweating. In another dream I managed to save Teacher Sarah, but when I woke up, I'd remember that I hadn't.

My sisters and I had many of the same fears, and they lingered for a long time. We were terrified of monkeys. To us they were not cute or cuddly animals, like Curious George. In Africa they often stole mangoes and bananas from the trees. We needed those fruits, especially when we ran out of other food. The monkeys even tried to steal mealie meal, cassava, or rice from our bowls. Because the squirrels in our front yard looked like monkeys, we were afraid of them too.

Dogs also scared us. Our family's dog, Alaska, had died of old age soon after we arrived in the US and we didn't get to know him well. When Mama took us shopping in the local mall, she'd take us to the pet shop so we'd get used to small animals. As long as the puppies were in their cages, we loved watching them.

~

One summer day, Adam took us to the mall. As usual we begged for a visit to the pet shop. We were admiring a cute little spotted puppy with floppy ears, when, without warning, the salesperson let it out of the cage so we could pet it.

We were wearing sandals, and the puppy began to yip and nip at our toes. Mia and I panicked. We took off together, running and screaming through the mall with our brother chasing us.

'Stop! Stop! Come back!' Adam shouted, but we kept going, afraid that the puppy was still chasing us.

When we finally turned back, we saw the police arresting Adam.

'Uh-oh! Adam's getting arrested,' Mia said.

'What happened?' I asked.

'I dunno, but we'd better go back and save him,' she advised.

One of the police officers came up to us. 'Are you little girls all right?' he asked us.

We weren't about to talk to a strange man. I remember standing there trembling until a policewoman came over and asked the same question. I felt more comfortable answering her when she asked, 'Where is your mother?'

'She's home,' I said.

'Are you girls here all by yourselves?' she asked.

'No, we're with our big brother,' Mia answered.

'Well, where is he?' she asked.

I pointed in Adam's direction. 'He's right there.'

'But the dog bit our toes, so we ran away from him,' Mia explained.

'From your brother?' the police officer asked.

'No, from the dog,' I said.

The policewoman brought us to Adam. 'Do you know this man?' she asked.

'Oh course,' I answered. 'That's Adam. He's our big brother.'

Mia wrapped her arms around Adam and begged him to take us to the food court, but he didn't. He took us right home. When he got there, he said to our mother, 'I will never, ever take them out in public again.' He did eventually take us out again, but first we had to promise never to run away from him.

We were still learning English and we didn't have a full vocabulary, so it was hard to explain to our family why we were so afraid of dogs. But one day, as I watched my papa shave, I figured out how to say it. My father had foamy white shaving cream on his face, and I said, 'You look like the mad dog that came to our orphanage one day.'

Papa didn't understand, so I took his can of shaving cream and squirted it onto my chin. Then I dropped to my hands and knees, growling and snapping my teeth as I showed him what happened when a dog growled at a group of us as we played soccer in the orphanage yard.

'Rabies!' Papa exclaimed. 'No wonder you girls are so afraid of dogs.'

~

Fireworks also frightened us. On our first Fourth of July in the United States, Papa and Mama took us to watch the fireworks. We didn't know what fireworks were, so Mama drew us each a picture of them and sprinkled glitter on them.

Mia and I carried our pictures to the field, where we were going to watch the fireworks. When it was dark, Papa pointed to the sky. I looked up, expecting to see glitter. What a shock it was to hear an explosion and see the real fireworks. 'Bombs! Bombs!' Mia and I screamed. I thought the war had followed us to America.

~

Eventually I stopped being afraid of squirrels, puppies and fireworks, but I was still afraid of humans. Nothing terrified me as much as the debils, who left mutilated bodies on the sides of the roads in my home country. In those early days of living in the United States, I saw debils everywhere, especially in the windows at night.

'Debils! Debils!' we screamed in those first nights in our new home, when we saw what were our own reflections or the reflections of our family members in our bedroom windows. I soon learned that there were no debils outside our second-storey bedroom window. But even today, I don't like bare windows at night. I still feel the need to close my blinds tightly after dark.

~

Mia, Mariel and I also hated camouflage clothing. We were convinced that every man who wore camouflage clothing was a debil. Once, we were so terrified of a group of soldiers from nearby Fort Dix that we ran across a car park and into a highway. The soldiers chased us and rounded us up. I thought that they were going to kill us, but instead they turned us over to our mother.

Another time our fear of camouflage ruined what could have been the perfect ending to a day of ballet. Mama and Papa had taken us to New York City to see the ballet. After the performance, we took too long to get to the cloakroom, and it was closed. Albert Evans, a principal dancer with the New York City Ballet, came to our rescue. He led us around the building in search of our coats. On the elevator he tried to strike up a conversation, but we were too terrified of him. Though I longed to talk to this famous ballet dancer, I didn't dare. He was wearing a blue camouflage parka, so I was convinced that he was a debil as well as a dancer. It upset me to think that a person who danced ballet might also kill me.

~

To this day, I am also afraid of loud male voices. The debils were loud, whether they were shouting in anger or laughing in victory. Many times, Mia, Mariel and I would run into the house and report to our parents that there was an African man outside. It wouldn't matter what colour he was. A shouting man was a debil.

Cheering fathers at a swim meet terrified me. Schoolteachers, ballet teachers, men on the street . . .

whether they were of Caucasian, African, Asian, Native American or Hispanic descent, it didn't matter. If I heard men shouting, I remembered the frightening voices of the debils on a rampage in my native Sierra Leone.

Chapter 18

Bigotry and Jealousy

At first I thought that nothing could be more wonderful than my life in the United States. My family loved me. My sisters and I got along well. I had friends. I had lots of fun dancing, playing and swimming. I believed that everything and everybody in this wonderful new country of mine was perfect. Though my parents and brothers were white, and my sisters and I were black, we didn't seem to care about skin colour. It never occurred to me that we should feel any other way, and I never suspected that anyone else would care. I didn't know anything about racial intolerance then, but I learned about it soon enough. I felt very sad when I experienced it in my neighbourhood, in restaurants and in shops. But I felt worse when I discovered it in the world of ballet.

My earliest experience of bigotry occurred in my own front yard. Mia and I were dressed in hand-me-down gowns, having a tea party on the lawn with our dolls, when a neighbour walked over and said, 'You girls will need to take your things and move your tea party out of sight of *my property*. I'm trying to sell my house. Someone is coming to look at it, and I don't want them to see the two of *you*.'

At the time I didn't understand that there was racial prejudice in America, so I was confused about why the neighbour didn't want anyone to see us. 'Are we ugly? Are we bad? Do we have grass stains on our clothes? Are we making too much noise?' Mia and I asked ourselves those questions and many more.

~

Not long after the neighbour asked us to move off our lawn, we had another experience almost like the first. While at the mall, Mia and I skipped ahead of our mother. Two white women passed us by and said, 'Tsk, look at them, running around loose in the mall like a couple of wild animals.'

Mia, Mariel and I heard many comments like this when we were little, and they hurt our feelings because we took them to heart.

Then, one afternoon, Mama and Papa stopped at the video shop and bought us the Disney movie *Ruby Bridges*. It was the story of how six-year-old Ruby Bridges led the crusade to integrate the schools in New Orleans. We watched it and were amazed by the idea of bigotry.

We talked about that movie with our parents afterwards. And it helped me understand that the discrimination we experienced had nothing to do with whether we were pretty or not, or whether we made noise, or had grass stains on our clothes. We could have been the most perfect children in the neighbourhood, but some people would still have hated us for the colour of our skin.

Ruby Bridges prepared us for an imperfect future. Now we understood why sales assistants in shops followed closely behind us and hovered over us while we shopped for clothes. We knew why they sometimes grabbed the clothes from our hands whenever we touched them. Once, when we were shopping for jeans, a white sales assistant told us to go shop where we belonged. Thanks to *Ruby Bridges*, we were not shocked by her behaviour.

This is not to say that all of our encounters with white people were tainted with prejudice. The movie taught us that there were many white people who were like our parents. They were not filled with hatred.

When Ruby Bridges's father lost his job, a white neighbour offered him another one. The teacher who volunteered to teach Ruby Bridges was a white woman. Some of the white people in her neighbourhood even walked behind the federal marshal's car when Ruby went to school.

Even though I understand the reason why it happens, I still feel uncomfortable in shops and restaurants when people stare at our family. We were with our parents a month or so when I began to forget that they were a different colour than I was. When I looked at their faces, I just saw Mama and Papa. However, when other people stared at us, I'd remember that we were different. It bothered me then and bothers me even more now when people make me feel this way.

Today I can almost see the wheels turning in people's heads as they try to figure out why two white senior citizens are with a group of black teens. Recently, when Mia and I were shopping with Mama, I had my arm over Mama's shoulder as she was opening her purse to give Mia her credit card. A white man came up to her and said, 'Ma'am, are you okay?'

It wasn't just white people who stared at us; it was black people as well. It wasn't just white people who showed us how racist they were. Black people often did that too.

Black women sometimes came up to Mama and told her that she wasn't raising us right because we didn't have hair extensions or straight parts in our hair. They sometimes criticised our parents because we had ashy skin from swimming in a chlorinated pool. Once, a lady asked my mother, 'What crazy social worker placed those girls with you?'

Papa thought it was funny that most of our experiences with racism happened in the car park of our supermarket, and usually involved women. He would make a joke of it. Before he'd let us out of the car in the car park, he would ask us, 'Did you lotion your arms and legs? Did you pick your hair? We don't want the nappy-hair-and-ashy-skin policewomen after us.' We'd giggle and think Papa was very funny, but we also knew what would await us if we weren't perfectly groomed, so we'd reach for the lotion and hair picks that Mama always left in the car.

Despite the clowning around, both my mother and my father took the racism seriously. They warned us that we would be judged more harshly than little white girls in everything that we did; all of our failures would be blamed on race. We believed them, so we worked hard at everything we did.

As we grew older, my sisters and I began to notice reports of racism in the newspapers, and they definitely changed the way we lived our lives. When I lived in Vermont, there were so many articles about the profiling of black drivers there that I was afraid to get my driver's licence. Also, in Vermont supermarkets, when my mother wanted to use her credit card, the cashier never asked for proof of ID when she was alone or with my father. If she were with me or one of my sisters, the cashier would always ask to see her ID.

While living in New York City, we read reports of racial profiling in upmarket stores, even reports of unwarranted searches and pat-downs of black shoppers. As a result, I am always very careful of my every move in those stores.

~

I noticed a unique type of racial distrust in the city. My mother and I must always look like we know where we are going in Manhattan, because people always stop us and ask for directions. Even if she and I are linked arm and arm, when a white person needs directions, she will always ask my mother for them. If a black person needs directions, she will always ask me.

When I'm with either one of my parents, who are now senior citizens, I'm often assumed to be their carer. When I use the laundry room in our apartment complex, the nannies will talk to me but they will never talk to my parents. The same thing happens with the white residents in the building, only in reverse. They'll talk to my parents, but not to me.

Sometimes an incident of bigotry might even be funny. My most humorous encounters come with a form of stereotyping. Often, upon learning that I am a dancer, someone will ask me, 'What kind of dancing do you do . . . hip-hop?' This makes my ballerina friends laugh. We all look alike: lean, long-legged, hair in a bun, and because of the rotation of our hips, our toes point out like ducks'. Why are they presumed to be ballerinas, but I am presumed to be a hip-hop artist?

Now that I'm older, I've learned to detach my personal feelings from the bigotry. I'm able to step back and look at it for what it is: a combination of fear and ignorance. Unless I'm in physical danger or my civil rights are being violated, I ignore it. I tell myself that it isn't worth getting worked up about it. However, there is one form of racial discrimination that I am unable to ignore, and that is the racial bias in the world of ballet.

Chapter 19

Where Are the Black Ballerinas?

I first recognised that there is racial inequality in ballet when I was only four years old and had watched that first video of *The Nutcracker*. I couldn't put it into complicated language at the time. I didn't know the words *bigotry*, *prejudice* or *discrimination*. I was only able to ask, 'Mama, where are the black ballerinas?'

When my parents took me to see the Pennsylvania Ballet's *Nutcracker*, I was happy to see not one, but two black ballerinas that day: Nikkia Parish and Heidi Cruz.

I noticed Meredith Rainey, a black male dancer there too, and I would eventually learn that black male ballet dancers were not so rare.

By the time I was eight years old, my parents had taken Mia, Mariel and me to see ballet in New York City as well as Philadelphia. I had seen performances of Philadanco, the Pennsylvania Ballet, the American Ballet Theatre and the Alvin Ailey American Dance Theater. By then I had been taking dance lessons for three years and understood the differences between dance styles.

I began peppering my parents with questions that they couldn't answer, such as, 'Why are there lots of black dancers in the contemporary companies, but not in the classical and neoclassical companies that tell the stories that I love so much?'

My mother promised to take me to a neoclassical company that had many black ballerinas. 'It's the Dance Theatre of Harlem,' she said, 'and it features the type of story ballets that you love.' I remember leaning over her shoulder, charged with excitement as she went online to buy tickets, and the disappointment that I felt when Mama said, 'Oh no! It's closed! Look, it says right here that the Dance Theatre of Harlem's professional company is no longer performing, because it lacks the money to continue.'

I felt a lump in my throat. 'Mama, where can a black ballerina dance in a classical?' I asked, but my mother didn't have an answer to my question.

There were many black kids, girls and boys, who attended the Rock School with me in Philadelphia, and soon I began to wonder what would happen when we grew up if there were hardly any black dancers in ballet companies. I decided that there had to be ballet companies that had black ballerinas other than contemporary companies. I found a list of ballet companies in a dance magazine and began my own research. I was determined to find those black women.

A friend of my mother had once told me that to get into the best black sororities in college, you had to have skin lighter than the brown bags used in supermarkets, and she had failed the 'brown-paper-bag test'. I thought about that a lot as day after day I searched through dozens of head shots on ballet company websites, hoping to find a smiling black face. I did find quite a few black male dancers, but rarely did I find a black female dancer, and those whom I did find were light enough to pass the brown-paper-bag test.

I began to question whether my skin colour would prevent me from becoming a ballet dancer. My self-doubts grew when I heard what people said about black ballerinas. That year, in *The Nutcracker*, I danced the part of a Polichinelle, one of the little doll-like figures that pop out from under Mother Ginger's skirt. During rehearsal one of the mothers who was chaperoning us said, 'Black girls just shouldn't be dancing ballet. They're too athletic. They should leave the classical ballet to white girls. They should stick to modern or jazz. That's where they belong.' My younger sister told me that she once heard a dance teacher claim, 'Black girls can't point their toes.'

Once, someone in the ballet world, whose opinion meant a lot to me said to my mother, 'We don't like to waste a lot of time, money and effort on the black girls. When they reach puberty, they develop big thighs and behinds, and can't dance ballet any more.' I overheard the remark, but I wasn't supposed to be outside the door listening in, so I couldn't speak up and challenge what he said. My mother did, though, and that made me feel a little better. However, those words still terrified me to the point that I worried endlessly about the fateful day when I'd reach puberty and grow a big butt and big thighs.

I was in an audience watching a performance of *Raymonda Variations* when I overheard a woman criticise a black ballerina, saying, 'She'll never make principal dancer; she isn't delicate enough. Black women are just too athletic for classical ballet. They're too muscular. That's why so few of them make it into companies.' I flexed my bicep and slid my right hand up my left arm. I gave it a quick squeeze, wondering if my muscles were too big.

Ms Stephanie, the co-director of the Rock School, made me feel better the next week when she said, 'If you keep working hard, I don't see any reason why you can't one day become a world-class dancer.'

I thought about that when the mother of one of my dance-school classmates said, 'Michaela has a lot of strength. She dances like a real brute. Black dancers just have that kind of body.'

I cried all the way home that night, at first refusing to tell my mother what was bothering me. Finally I blurted out, 'Do I dance like a brute?'

My mother told me the mean comments that I overheard about black ballerinas were based on jealousy as well as bigotry.

'You need to ignore them,' she said.

'But I can't!' I sobbed as I struggled to catch my breath. 'I'm worried that I'll never be a ballerina.'

My mother's words couldn't comfort me, because I was her daughter and I knew that she would think I was perfect and beautiful, even if I were ugly, too athletic, and danced like a brute. Therefore, she couldn't make me believe that the comments were about someone else's prejudice and jealousy, and were definitely not true. It took a professional ballerina to convince me of that.

One day I stood outside of my ballet class crying quietly because I didn't want anyone to notice me. We had auditioned for the summer ballet intensive programme the week before, and I had skipped a level. A group of mothers went to the director to complain about my placement. Before class they had been whispering together and pointing at me in the lobby. Now I had to face their daughters, and I was afraid to go into class.

My crying wasn't as secretive as I had hoped. As I

stood alone in the hallway, Heidi Cruz happened to walk by just then. She saw me crying and stopped. I had no idea if she knew who I was, but she made me explain why I was so upset.

'Michaela, you are a very talented young dancer,' she said. 'And you're going to meet many jealous people. Don't let them take you down. Just hold your head up. Look straight ahead and ignore them, or they will destroy you. Believe me; I know. The same thing happened to me when I was your age.'

It had never occurred to me before that I wasn't the first ballerina to suffer this way, and I will always be grateful to Heidi for helping me that day. Knowing that she had experienced the same thing buoyed my spirits. I followed her advice, and I'm glad that I did, because as I grew older, life got harder and more complicated. I didn't need something as trivial as jealousy to bring me down.

Jealousy is a big factor in the world of ballet. There were millions of girls taking ballet lessons and far too few jobs available in companies. The competition to get into these companies is real and starts when they are very young. I had to learn to cope with it, or it would destroy my spirit and hold me back from reaching my goals.

I didn't do this immediately. It took a long time for me to learn how to ignore the jealousy and bigotry that would enter my life. At that age I was very confused by the fact that mothers got into their daughters' business. It was hard enough to deal with the jealousy of the other kids, without their parents being involved in it too.

It was the parents who often started the meanest rumours. One rumour that spread like wildfire was that my mother had cut three years off my age so that everyone would think that I was very talented. This one upset me more than any other, and I responded to it in my usual way, by bottling it up until I exploded in tears on the way home.

'Why would parents be jealous of me? That just doesn't make any sense,' I cried, trying to wrap my mind around it.

My mother explained to me how some parents try to live through their children's experiences. 'If a mother wanted to be a ballerina and couldn't do it, sometimes she tries to live her life through her daughter. That causes her to feel jealousy towards you if she perceives that you are a better dancer than her daughter.'

'Will they do it for ever?' I asked as I tried to wipe my tears with a crumbling tissue.

She told me that nothing lasted for ever. 'There will come a day when these girls will no longer be a part of your life, and you'll no longer care about what they once said about you.'

Chapter 20

Dancing *The Nutcracker*!

My parents explained to us that when the debils attacked Mariel's village, they had killed her father and shot off her then-pregnant mother's leg. As a result, Mariel was born too early. Her early birth, plus the lead poisoning, malaria and malnutrition that we all had suffered in the orphanage, affected her the worst and made it hard for her to learn now.

I was just wild about ballet classes from the moment that I stepped into the Rock School. Mia saw how much I liked it and eventually asked to change to the Rock School as well. Mariel wasn't a bit interested in ballet, but soon after we adopted her, she insisted on taking lessons, because she didn't want to wait in the lobby while Mia and I were in class. So, when I returned to the Rock School at age seven, Mia and Mariel came along too.

When I entered Level 2, my first pointe class, Mia entered Level 1X, the level right behind me and Mariel entered Level 1. I soon noticed that Mia and I were making real progress, but Mariel would fall asleep at the barre and couldn't seem to learn the basic steps and combinations that were taught in her level.

Mariel wasn't just slow in ballet. Despite the fact that she was only four months younger than me and eight months younger than Mia, she was behind us in nearly everything. When we were younger and in the orphanage, Mia and I hadn't noticed this so much, but now that we were older, it was obvious to us.

Even though ballet was so difficult for Mariel and not much fun for her either, she stuck with it because she wanted to dance in *The Nutcracker* with the Pennsylvania Ballet. You had to be eight years old to dance in *The Nutcracker*, so in my first year back at the Rock School, both Mariel and I, who were seven, couldn't audition.

As I waited in the lobby of the dance school, I looked on with envy as Mia and all of my classmates went up into the dance studio to audition. I learned a lesson from just observing that year, when some kids came down smiling and others came down crying. It's a lesson that I have never forgotten – you don't always get the role that you hope for.

At that time there weren't a lot of little boys taking ballet, so some of the girls had been cast as Party Boys. They were often the ones crying. It seemed that nobody wanted to be a Party Boy.

My stomach twisted into knots as I waited for Mia to come down. She was very tall for eight and her hair was short, and even though I was jealous that she was older than me, I still wanted the best for her. So I worried the whole time that she wouldn't be cast in the envied role of a Party Girl.

When Mia entered the lobby, she was grinning from ear to ear. I raced up to her, and breathless with excitement, I asked, 'What did you get?'

Mia's violet-brown eyes sparkled with joy when she exclaimed, 'I'm a Party Boy and a Mouse!'

And so, from my sister, I learned the second half of that lesson. If you don't want the role you got, there's always another dancer who does.

~

Mia loved dancing in *The Nutcracker* that year. Mama and Papa took Mariel and me to see the show several times, and each time I felt just as excited as the last as I watched and longed for my turn. But there were many months of hard work ahead before the next *Nutcracker* audition, and soon the holiday season was over and we were back to work in the dance studio.

The Rock School is what is known as a syllabus school. That means it has a list of dance steps and combinations of dance steps that you have to learn at each level to move on to the next level. For example, in Level 1, you might be expected to do a combination of dance steps like: tendu to second, relevé, demi-plié, return to first. But in Level 3X you would be expected to do a combination like: fondu front en relevé, close; fondu back, inside leg en relevé, close; fondu outside leg to second en relevé, then plié with the standing leg while the working leg is at forty-five degrees, then go to passé. Repeat in reverse.

Students didn't move up from level to level without being ready. Everybody had different muscle strength, coordination and basic ability, so some kids spent one year in a level, and others spent two or three years in a level before moving up.

At the end of that year, Mia and I danced in the Rock School's summer intensive, which was an all-day ballet programme, and we'd hurry home at the end of the programme to our swim team practice. Swimming had become nearly, but not quite, as important to me as ballet.

In the autumn Mia and I learned that we had each been moved up to the next level in ballet, but Mariel had not changed levels. She remained in Level 1, and she was very disappointed because her best friends in Level 1 had moved up to Level 1X without her.

On the way home from class, Mia and I couldn't

contain our excitement over our new ballet levels until we heard Mariel sniffling.

'Mariel, do you want to be a ballerina when you grow up?' I asked her. 'If you do, I'll tutor you at home.'

'Of course I don't!' she answered, with a pout on her face. 'I want to be a babysitter.'

'Then why are you taking ballet lessons?' I asked. 'Because I want to be in *The Nutcracker*,' she answered. 'Well, you're eight years old now, and you can be in *The Nutcracker*. Level 1 kids are the angels.'

'Whew! That's a relief,' Mariel admitted. 'I really didn't want to move up to Level 1X, because ballet is too hard for me. I'd rather play drums.'

~

On the day of *The Nutcracker* auditions, I knew that Mariel's days as a ballerina were limited. I just prayed that she'd get chosen to be an angel. I wanted her to have the thrilling experience of performing in *The Nutcracker* at least one time. After her audition Mariel came into the lobby glowing like the star on the top of a Christmas tree. She had been cast as an angel.

Mia had shot up like a sunflower during the past year, and she knew that she was now too tall to be a child in the party scene. She worried that she'd be too tall for the role of a Polichinelle, nicknamed Polly, who pops out from under Mother Ginger's Dress and yet she was too young to be cast as a Hoop. 'Do you think I'm too tall to be a Polly?' she'd ask me every night before we fell asleep.

I'd answer, 'No, I think you'll be a Polly.' Then I'd fall asleep, hoping that I wouldn't be wrong, and Mia wouldn't be disappointed.

Thankfully, Mia was cast as a boy Polly and a Mouse. I was cast as a girl Polly and a Party Girl in Cast A. I would be dancing about forty times, and half of them with Mia.

I remember how nervous and excited I felt about dancing my first role in a professional ballet. I couldn't even sleep the night before we opened, and I had butterflies in my stomach before I stepped onto the stage. But when the orchestra began playing, I was suddenly calm. I was no longer Michaela. I was a different girl, one of several friends of Marie, who are attending her family's holiday party in Victorian England.

That holiday season, our lives revolved around *The Nutcracker*. We listened to the music every day in rehearsal and later in performances. As though that wasn't enough Tchaikovsky for one season, Mia taught herself to play *The Nutcracker Suite* on the piano at home, and played it endlessly. Mama baked nutcracker sugar cookies that filled the house with delicious smells. From that year on, the sound of the introduction to *The*

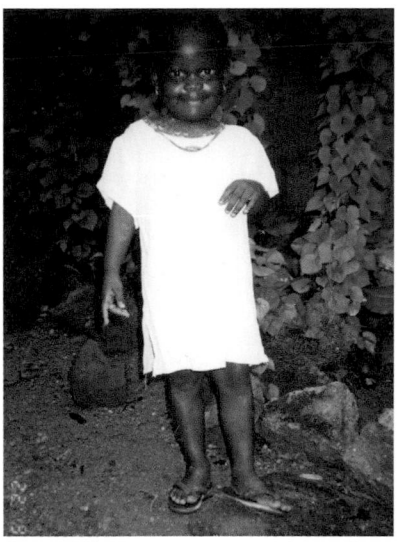

Despite having a belly and face swollen by malnutrition at age three and a half, I'm standing happy and proud because an American visitor just painted my fingernails.

This dress was a hand-me-down donation, but at the time, it was the prettiest dress I had ever seen. The grass mat beneath my feet is the sleeping mat that I shared with Mia.

The children from our orphanage at the safe house in Guinea (I'm at the far left, in front of Mia).

After escaping Sierra Leone, we arrived at this bleak United Nations refugee camp in Guinea before moving to the safe house.

Inside the plastic hut at the refugee camp (I'm at the far left). When we got there, we were all hungry and covered with chickenpox.

Here we are piled in a car leaving the refugee camp
for the safe house in Guinea.

Mariel, Mia, and me (from left to right), with another child,
waiting patiently for our visas after arriving in Ghana.

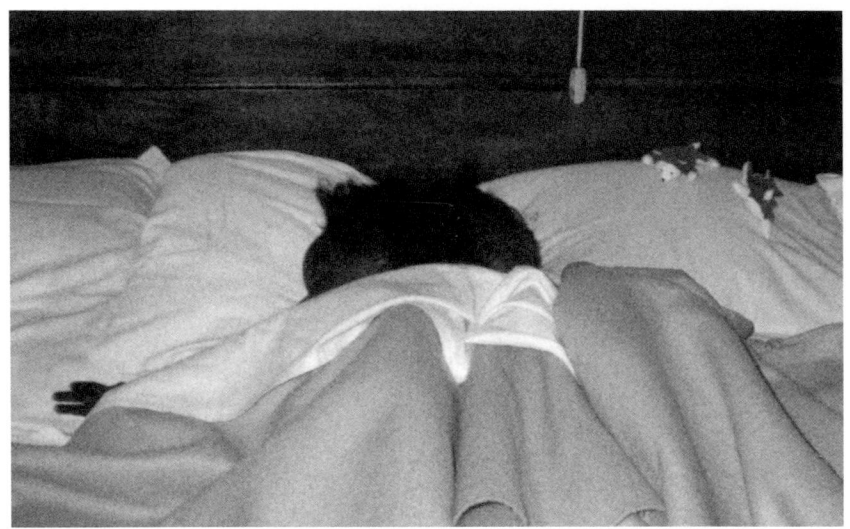

At the hotel room in Ghana, Mia and I slept in a real bed with pillows and blankets for the first time. We snuggled together the way we did on our grass mat at the orphanage, in spite of all the space.

At age four, just a few weeks after arriving in the United States, Mia and I already looked healthier.

Our new brother Teddy delighting Mia and me by tossing us around.

My mother finally let me hold Baby Emma on her last day with us.

Teddy teaching me how to eat spaghetti for the first time.

Papa and me on my first carousel ride at the Jersey Shore.

Teddy took us trick-or-treating in angel costumes
Mama made for us on our first Halloween.

Mia and me, in the turkey dresses that Mama made for us,
with Papa on our first Thanksgiving.

Mia shared her fifth birthday with me because
I had never had a birthday cake before, and
she even let me blow out some candles.

Mama and me riding
the tram to the top of
Mt Killington in Vermont.

Mama reading a bedtime story to Mia and me, as she did every night.

Mia was good-natured enough to always dance the role of the boy when we performed our version of the party scene from *The Nutcracker*.

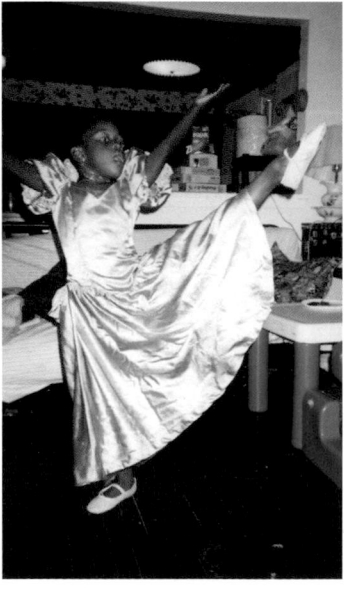

At age five, I liked to wear hand-me-down dresses and pretend that I was dancing in a ballet.

Such a happy day! Mia and me kissing Papa when our adoption was finalised.

Mia and me, at age seven, with Mariel and Mama
on our way to see the New York City Ballet.

Mia, Mariel, and I choreographed a dance to perform together for our parents.

Mia, me, and Mariel (from left to right) wearing the blue ribbons
we won in the swimming medley relay.

By age eight, I already wanted to dance wherever I went.
Here I'm at Shenandoah National Park in Virginia.

Practising arabesques in my bedroom,
wearing my new pointe shoes.

This is my first formal ballet photo.
Luckily, you can't see the stains from the
chocolate bar that melted all over my
tights on the way to the studio.

Papa, Mama, Mariel, Mia, me, and Amie (from left to right) celebrating the finalisation of Amie's adoption.

Me, at age twelve, with Jestina, Mia, and Bernice (from left to right), singing and dancing while on vacation in California.

Dancing at the pool after breaking the Tri-County Swimming League backstroke record.

Leaping over Mia in the dance I choreographed
to the music from *Pirates of the Caribbean.*

Bernice, Mia, Mariel, me, and Jestina (from left to right)
in our holiday photo, when I was thirteen.

During this photo shoot in Johannesburg, South Africa, when I danced for the Joburg Ballet, I worried that the pigeons would have little respect for the beautiful costume. Fortunately, they left it alone!

Reviewing footage for *First Position*, the ballet documentary I was featured in, with the movie's director, Bess Kargman.

The movie poster for *First Position*.

Mama and me in Los Angeles for my appearance on *Dancing with the Stars*.

Being interviewed on *Dancing with the Stars* by host Tom Bergeron.

(top right) The magazine cover that I found as an orphan in Sierra Leone, which inspired me to become a ballerina.

(bottom right) Dancing in *Le Corsaire* with the Joburg Ballet.

(left) Dancing the role of the Black Swan in *Swan Lake* with the Dance Theatre of Harlem.

Nutcracker Suite would overwhelm me with excitement and warm holiday feelings.

Mariel danced her one and only *Nutcracker* performance that year. She did a perfect job of it, despite the fact that, one day, she ran a fever shortly before the performance and vomited all over the stage while dancing. She was so professional about it that no one even noticed. However, when those in the role of Chocolate from Spain danced on after the angels, one of the dancers slipped on the stage and wrinkled his nose with disgust at the smell.

At the end of the season, Mariel said, 'I think I'm going to quit ballet. Being in *The Nutcracker* was a lot harder than I thought it would be.'

Chapter 21

Turning a Blind Eye

In January only Mia and I returned to the Rock School. By the following *Nutcracker* season, I had skipped a level. I was nine years old and in Level 3X. Mia had just turned ten years old in September, and she was in Level 3. Though we were only four months apart, I looked like a little kid and Mia now looked like a teenager.

During the war in Sierra Leone, Mia had been hit on the head and knocked unconscious. The injury was so severe that she had no memory of it, but it caused damage to her pituitary gland, and caused her body to grow and mature too early.

She knew that she was now too tall to dance the role of a Polly.

The Nutcracker audition was particularly stressful that year. There had been talk of my being cast as Marie, and I was especially anxious. At the audition I learned that I would not be Marie. *Don't cry in front of everyone, Michaela,* I told myself as I struggled to hold back my tears. I asked permission to use the bathroom. There I let the tears flow and quickly wiped them away so that I could return to the audition.

As I opened the door to leave the bathroom, two adults passed by. I quickly shut it again when I heard one of them say, 'Why not Michaela DePrince? She's perfect for Marie.' I nudged it open an inch, just in time to hear the other person say, 'Because this city isn't ready for a black Marie.' I stood frozen by the door, wondering if the city or the world would ever be ready for a black Marie, or a black Sugar Plum Fairy.

Despite my disappointment, I was excited when both Mia and I were cast as Hoops. But after casting most of the Pollys, the casting director then noticed that none of them had experience with that role. Without at least one experienced Polly to lead the way, this dance could become a disaster.

The director looked at his Hoops. I was the youngest and smallest, so he pulled me out of Hoops and took me aside. 'Michaela, I hate to do this to you, but I desperately need you to guide the Pollys. Would you mind being a Polly for one more year? I'll make it up to you next year.'

'Not at all. I'll dance whatever role you need me to dance,' I answered with a brave face, even though I wanted to burst into tears. So that year I was a Polly and a Mouse. I reminded myself that I'd be dancing ballet for many years, and there was plenty of time to get a choice role. Now, when I look back on it, I'm glad that Mia got the role of a Hoop, because that was the last time she ever danced in a professional ballet production.

~

Mia moved into Level 3X the following year and hated the fact that she would need to take classes six days a week. Her true love was her piano, and she worried that she wasn't getting enough practice. I suspected that soon Mia would quit ballet. For years we had done everything together. I dreaded that we might be going our separate ways.

Finally the day came when Mia said, 'Mama, I like ballet, but not six times a week. I miss my piano. I want to take piano lessons two or three times a week, instead of once.'

My heart leaped into my throat when Mia said that. I waited for my mother's response and hoped that she would say, 'No way!' Instead Mama asked, 'Are you sure?'

'No! She's not sure!' I cried out.

'Michaela! What's wrong with you? Mama's asking me, not you. I'm not your identical twin. For me ballet is fun and exercise, until it gets in the way of my piano playing. Then it's not fun any more,' Mia explained.

Then she turned to Mama and said, 'I've been thinking about this for a long time, and I'm absolutely sure.'

My relationship with Mia was different from my relationship with Mariel or Amie, a Liberian teenager whom my family had adopted the year before. Mia and I were much closer. I had assumed that we would do everything together our whole lives. At night, when we lay in bed, we'd plan how we'd marry brothers and buy houses next door to each other. In that moment I saw all those dreams crashing down around me. I felt like Mia was abandoning me.

'At least we'll still swim together,' Mia assured me. And the summer that she quit ballet, it seemed that, whenever I wasn't dancing, she and I were at the pool together swimming. When we were eight years old, we had both been part of our swim club's relay team. Together, with two of our teammates, we broke a league record in the eight-and-under relay. Now, at ten years old, Mia, Mariel and I would often take the first-, second- and third-place ribbons for our age division at the summer meets. That was the summer when I broke two individual league records, one in the butterfly and the other in the backstroke. My coach used to tease that I was fast because I swam with my toes pointed like a ballerina's.

139

I used to swim without goggles, but the year before I broke the record I started wearing them because I was having trouble seeing the end of my lane. I also began bumping into other students in my ballet class. This happened most frequently when I was doing piqué turns across the room. 'Michaela, are you spotting?' my teacher would ask. *Spotting* means continuously keeping an eye on a distant point as you turn. If you don't spot, you turn like a wobbly top. I had learned to spot when I was five or six years old. I was insulted that the teacher thought that, at nine, I couldn't spot.

'Yes, I'm spotting,' I answered.

'You don't look like you are,' he said. 'You're staggering like a drunken sailor as you travel across the floor, and you're knocking your classmates off balance when you bump into them.'

That night I tried to spot while crossing my bedroom. I was fine when I turned to the right, but I couldn't seem to spot when I turned to the left. 'I think I need glasses,' I said to my mother. 'My vision is a little fuzzy in my left eye.' She made an appointment for me with the eye doctor.

While I waited for my turn at the doctor's office, I admired a pair of Harry Potter frames. 'Can I get my eyeglass prescription filled today?' I asked the optician.

'It depends on your prescription, but we can probably fill it today.'

I handed her the Harry Potter frames, and she put them aside for me. Then I was called in to have my eyes examined. Our optometrist spent a lot of time chatting with us, asking about school and ballet, but I wanted her to hurry that day. I was excited about going on holiday to the beach later that afternoon.

The doctor took a look at my eye and gasped. I nearly jumped out of the chair when she did that. Then she called my mother over and showed her my eye through a magnifying glass. Mama gasped too. Then she started to cry. She was always totally matter-of-fact about medical problems, so when she cried, I got nervous. 'What's wrong?' I exclaimed, thinking that any second I would be crying too.

The vision in my left eye wasn't just fuzzy. It was almost gone. I had some kind of blister on my eye. The doctor thought that I had transferred a herpes cold sore from my lip to my eyeball, but I hadn't had a cold sore on my lip for years. The next thing I knew, I was on my way to the emergency room without the cool Harry Potter glasses.

The doctor ordered blood tests, and when the results came back, we all got a big surprise. I had never recovered from the mononucleosis that I had contracted in Africa when I was four years old. My blood work showed that I still had a very bad infection after five years! The ophthalmologist had never heard of this. She immediately put me on an antiviral drug. The drug was designed to treat the herpes virus. She didn't know for sure if it would work on the Epstein–Barr virus, which was the kind that had caused my mononucleosis, but eventually the blister on my eye healed, and I stopped bumping into my classmates in ballet class.

~

My family did get to the beach for our holiday that summer. My big brother Teddy drove to the seashore and joined us for a few days. I literally screamed with joy when he showed up. Teddy rode with me on the go-carts and let me steer. Once I had my fill of the go-carts, my sisters and I ran along the beach, watching Teddy parasail by in the sky over the water.

That autumn, after a glorious summer, I returned to my ballet lessons at the Rock School. My life was busy with home-schooling, ballet lessons and *Nutcracker* rehearsals. I didn't worry about my eye too much. Actually, the only time I thought about it at all was when I needed to spot and when my mother dropped medicine into my eye at night. Besides, something much more dramatic was happening in my life . . . in all of our lives that year. It was a drama that was far more serious than my eye.

Chapter 22

Loss

Teddy was my hero, and often my fellow mischief maker in our family. When Mia and I were very little, he'd play children's songs on the piano for us. When he'd bring his girlfriends home to meet us, he would carry us around on his shoulders and get us all wound up. Soon we'd be dancing and jumping all over the place like wild girls. He'd play circus with us, tossing us into the air and swinging us around.

'Mama! Papa! Look!' we'd shriek with mad delight. 'What's this *Papa* and *Mama* about?' he'd tease. 'Do you live in the woods with Goldilocks and the three bears? You need to say, *Mom* and *Dad*, like me.' So, because of Teddy's teasing, we eventually began sounding more like American kids.

Teddy loved to take us to the cinema. My parents would always warn him not to buy us fizzy drinks, but he'd buy us each a huge bucket of popcorn and an extra-large soft drink anyway. He spoiled us, and we knew it.

Teddy taught me how to eat spaghetti in America. He said that I should hold it high above my head and suck one strand down at a time. He even showed me the kind of sucking noise I should make, and he demonstrated how I should make very loud, slurpy sounds when I ate soup in a restaurant.

'Teddy! You're behaving worse than the little kids!' Mom would complain, but Dad just laughed at his antics.

Teddy came to all of our ballet showcases and piano recitals. He attended many of our swim meets, especially the championship meets. When Mia, Mariel and I were in *The Nutcracker*, Teddy was there. He was the cool, fun brother I never knew I wanted until I was lucky enough to have him. But my high-spirited brother slowly began losing his energy.

By the time he was twenty-three and I was nine, I began to recognise how sick Teddy was. The possibility of losing him took me by surprise, though it probably shouldn't have. When we were old enough to understand, my parents told us that they had lost two sons to haemophilia, a bleeding disorder. The blood that they used to treat the boys' haemophilia had been contaminated with HIV when they were little, and they developed AIDS. Cubby died at the age of eleven, nearly two years before I was born, and Michael died nine months after Cubby, when he was fifteen. Even though I saw their pictures on the wall above our fireplace, they didn't seem real to me . . . but Teddy, well, he was real – a dear and precious part of my daily life.

I was used to the idea of Teddy's having haemophilia. I often saw him injecting himself with his medicine. To him this was a common occurrence, no different from taking vitamins was to me. Though I had heard the words *haemophilia* and *HIV* many times, I never connected his illness to the thought of his dying.

In the autumn following our great summer at the beach, Teddy grew weaker and weaker. Soon he was barely able to walk. He was twenty-four years old and owned his own house by then, but he'd often sleep overnight at our home in the spare bedroom on the first floor. Often he'd spend the day resting on our huge leather sofa, just so that he could watch us play and listen to our conversations, interrupting often to tease us.

Our noise never bothered him. Teddy would claim that we were so funny that we made him feel better. Usually he fell asleep amid our chaos.

On the day my new sister Amie's adoption was finalised in court, we went out to dinner, but Teddy was too weak and tired to join us. On our way home Mom's mobile rang. It was Teddy, and I thought that he was calling to congratulate Amie. I expected Mom to pass the telephone to her, but she didn't. Instead I heard her say, 'Okay, we're almost home. We'll drop off the girls, and then Dad and I will drive right over to get you.'

'Are you picking up Teddy and bringing him over? Is he going to celebrate with us? Will he sleep over tonight?' I asked, but Mom didn't answer me. Instead she ignored my questions and continued talking to Teddy on the phone in a soft, quiet, calming voice the entire way home.

When we pulled into the driveway, Mom said, 'Teddy's sick. Your dad and I are going to take him to the hospital. You girls go inside and change into your pyjamas. You can watch television until we get home.'

My dinner did somersaults in my stomach. 'Can I come, please?' I begged.

'Can I come too?' Mia asked.

'No one is going except your mother and me,' Dad said.

Amie, Mia, Mariel and I sat cuddled on the sofa, trembling and whimpering like scared kittens. We were too worried and distracted to watch TV as we waited for hours to hear from our parents.

Finally the telephone rang. Mia and I ran to answer it. We pressed our faces close together so that we could both hear. 'We're on our way home, girls. We'll be there in ten minutes,' Mom said.

'How's Teddy?' we both asked at the same time.

'Is he coming home with you?' Mia asked.

'Do you want us to turn on his electric blanket to warm up his bed?' I asked.

'No,' Mom said.

'Is he okay?' I asked.

'We'll talk about it when I get home,' Mom answered. 'We're almost there.'

Mom and Dad put their arms around us when they got home and led us to the living room. Then, in a soft, shivery voice, Mom simply said, 'Girls, Teddy died tonight.'

I thought that my heart would break into a million pieces. I heard a loud scream in my head and realised that it was my own voice. All of my sisters screamed too. Our cries were loud, howling wails. Mariel rolled on the floor, hysterical with anguish. Mia and I clutched each other desperately. Amie threw herself into our mother's arms. Mom and Dad reached out and filled their arms with all of us, holding us close in a circle of comfort and love. It seemed to me that my parents had octopus arms, because they were able to wrap all of us together, but they couldn't hold our broken hearts together.

That day I felt such a pain in my chest that I thought my poor broken heart was bleeding. I had never before felt that sad, not even in Africa. But perhaps I was too young to remember exactly how I felt in Africa. Or perhaps I hadn't understood back then, when I was a tiny child, that death was for ever.

Now that I knew that death could snatch away my loved ones even in America, I began to worry about everyone in my family, especially my parents. The thought of losing them terrified me. I was so afraid that I would lose them that I tried to pull my affections away from them, reasoning that it wouldn't hurt me as much when they died.

What was worse, I pulled away from my sister Mia as well. Mia had been the one constant in my life for many years. She had been my first real friend and only real ally in the orphanage. Yet now I rejected her too. We began arguing constantly, and I stopped confiding in her like I used to do.

I learned from the loss of Teddy that people have different ways of dealing with grief. I know now that I chose a painful way of coping with his loss. Amie and I rebelled and held all of our loved ones at arm's length, while Mia and Mariel drew closer within the circle of family.

In the time after Teddy's death, I didn't really understand my feelings. My mom tried to help me and even insisted that I see a therapist to sort out my feelings, but I refused. Unless I was carried kicking and screaming out of the house, there was no way anybody would get me to see a therapist.

I was driving my parents crazy, but they never gave up on me. They never stopped loving me, even when I rebuffed their affection. Even in my mixed-up state of emotional confusion, that brought me comfort.

I think that there might have been a second reason why I was angry with my parents. I felt that they hadn't kept Teddy safe, which of course wasn't at all true. They had done as much for my brother as was humanly possible. But I felt that if they couldn't keep him safe and well, then how would they protect me? For a very long time after he died, my anger over this got me into situations from which I needed to be rescued . . . perhaps to prove to myself that my parents would save me, even though they hadn't been able to save Teddy.

Chapter 23
Moving On

Even though our home was filled with so many noisy girls, it seemed much sadder and lonelier without Teddy. Mia, Mariel, Amie and I began knitting when I was eight years old. I was nearly ten when Teddy died, and we were still knitting. We'd sit together at night, knitting and chatting before we went to bed. A couple of days after Teddy died, I held up a soft, thick grey scarf that I had been working on and asked, 'What should I do with this? I was knitting it to go with Teddy's favourite hoodie. I wanted to give it to him for Hanukkah.'

'Maybe you should finish it and give it to Daddy,' Mia suggested.

'No, it would make him too sad,' I said. 'And I can't give it to either one of our other brothers. They know I was knitting it for Teddy.'

'Then maybe you can finish it and give it to your favourite dance teacher,' Amie said.

'No, it's Teddy's. I can't do that,' I said. So instead I

just kept knitting and knitting. I took out the scarf whenever I felt sad and knitted more and more of it until it was nearly as long as my bedroom. It was my way of dealing with the sorrow of missing Teddy. And I probably would have knitted that scarf for ever if the shop hadn't run out of matching wool.

~

Less than two years after Teddy died, my family decided to move to Vermont. My parents had lived there when they were first married, and they said, 'All of our memories of Vermont are happy ones. We've lost three sons in New Jersey. We have too many sad memories here.'

My sisters and I agreed that a change might be good for all of us, especially because our parents decided that instead of home-schooling, Mia, Mariel and I could start sixth grade in a regular public school.

On our first morning in Vermont, we ate hot, fluffy pancakes with real maple syrup, something we could rarely find in New Jersey diners. Then we searched for a new home, one free of sad memories.

Soon we found the perfect home in Williston. It was close to the new dance school that I would attend and only a short distance from a piano teacher for Mia. When we went to visit it, I spotted a picturesque library standing close to Williston Central School. My parents agreed that we could visit the library while they saw the nearby house.

At the library I met a group of friendly girls. They introduced themselves to my sisters and me. Some of these girls would be in my sixth-grade class that autumn, if we bought the house.

The girls told us how lucky we'd be because it was on the bike path. They told us that depending on the season, we could walk, ski, snowshoe or ride our bicycles back and forth to the school and its playground, playing fields and ice-skating rink. I began to look forward to the fun I would have there, even though I was still sad to leave my friends and my ballet school behind.

Every time I felt sad about moving, I'd think of how painful it was to celebrate birthdays and holidays in our New Jersey home now that Teddy was gone. Every room was full of memories of him. He had such a huge personality; he had especially filled the kitchen, dining room and family room with his smiles and laughter. The mall, the parks, the cinema, the restaurants . . . his memory was everywhere I went. We all talked about this, and I knew that it was important for my family to start fresh somewhere else.

~

Before we moved to Vermont, I came up with a plan to leave my mark on New Jersey. I decided that I wanted to break the Tri-County Swimming League's fifty-metre girls' backstroke record for my team.

When they called my race at my last meet, I jumped into the pool, gripped the edge of it with my fingers and curled my legs in front of me with my feet pressed firmly against the wall. I shot off the wall at the bang of the starter's pistol, and slipped headfirst under the water. I came up stroking hard and fast, and could hear the crowd cheering.

When my fingertips touched the wall, I stood and looked around to see who had won. I burst into tears when I discovered that I was the only one standing there. I had beaten the next swimmer by a couple of body lengths. Those cheers had been for me. I had succeeded in breaking the record! That moment of triumph was my final memory of my life in New Jersey.

Even though I loved swimming, and the thrill of competition, it didn't make my heart soar like ballet did. Ballet was taking up more and more of my time, so it was getting harder and harder to find the time to fit in swim practice.

Also, I was petite, compact and small-boned. On looking at X-rays of my knee and wrist, a doctor had once predicted that I would grow to a full height of sixty-three to sixty-five inches. That is a wonderful height if I aspired to become a prima ballerina, but it wasn't tall enough if I wanted to become an Olympic swimmer. I began to notice that more and more of my competitors towered over me, standing several inches taller and outweighing me by about fifty pounds each. By sixth grade I was still wearing children's sizes in clothes, and they were nearly full-grown women.

I had to face the fact that I did not have the body of an Olympic swimmer, and I would not grow into one. In a way I was relieved because now I could dedicate myself to ballet without feeling too guilty about quitting swimming.

And after all, I was absolutely passionate about ballet!

Chapter 24

Growing Apart

'Why don't you stand up for me? Why do you always side with your new friends?' Mia cried as we walked home from school one day. '*Your friends* are mean to me! *You* are mean to me!' she shrieked as she hobbled with blood pouring from the cut on her knee. When she had fallen on a rock, a group of kids had laughed.

'My friends are *not* mean!' I shouted back at her. 'You're the one who's mean. You ignore them when they try to be nice to you.'

'Nice? Nice?' my sister sputtered. 'They're not trying to be nice. They make fun of me and talk about me when I can hear them.'

We hadn't been going to our new school for very long before it became evident that Mia and I were going our different ways. We had chosen to be in the same home-room, or 'house', as they called it at our school, because we had always been the very best of friends. I was getting to be more popular, though, because I could do things like a grand jeté and because the other kids thought that whatever I said was funny.

Mia, on the other hand, was shyer, quieter and much more serious than me. She was every bit as talented as I was, but in the eyes of sixth- and seventh-grade girls, classical piano and oboe weren't nearly as cool as ballet. Also, for a reason that I didn't understand, the most popular sixth-grade girls took an instant dislike to her. Now I realise that it was probably because she is gorgeous. The boys drooled over her, even though she wasn't very interested in them then.

Mariel was in a different house at school. She had different friends, and as a special-education student, she was more protected by the staff, which looked out for the kids with learning differences. But no one looked out for Mia in school, not even me.

Mia had defended me and protected me when we were in the orphanage in Africa, but when she needed the same protection, I wasn't there for her. I am sad to admit, that at the age of eleven, it was more important for me to be popular than to be a good friend to my sister.

At that time I didn't realise how much she was suffering. The boys were making inappropriate comments to her, and I ignored the situation. She finally got up the courage to complain to the headteacher in our school. The boys were called down to a meeting with him, and they admitted to their wrongdoing.

This got the boys off Mia's case, and many of them then befriended her, but now the girls really didn't like her for getting some of the most popular boys in trouble. Looking back on this, I realise that this was all typical middle school angst, but I was just a typical middle school kid, so I was acting like one.

Once again I sided against my sister, complaining about her getting *my* friends in trouble. I know now that what I should have said was 'I've got your back, Mia.' Just like she had my back in the orphanage.

For me the first term of middle school was a delight, whereas for Mia it was a nightmare. I was doing well in my classes. I was having a wonderful time and making friends at my new ballet school. When the cast list was posted for *The Nutcracker* production, I was overjoyed to see that I had been cast in seven roles. Then on a snowy evening in January, shortly before my twelfth birthday, I fell down the icy steps of the dance studio and everything changed.

I had been used to the ways of the Rock School, where the teachers didn't want an injured student dancing. There, an injured dancer would watch class until she felt well enough to dance again. I asked for a note from my mother and returned to my new class the next day. The teacher glanced at the note, grunted, and shoved it into his pocket. Then he pointed to the barre and commanded, 'Dance.' With great effort, I lifted my leg, but it went only as high as the lower of the two barres. The teacher walked by, grabbed my leg, and pulled it up to 180 degrees – until my toes pointed to the ceiling.

I was in so much pain that I dropped to the floor, squealing like an injured puppy. 'Here, we work through injuries,' the teacher said. I could barely walk to my mom's car that evening, and I never returned to that dance school again. Suddenly I no longer had a place to dance ballet.

~

As lost as I was without my ballet school, good things did happen as a result of my injury. I actually began to grow closer to Mia again. We began taking classes together at a new dance studio that had opened nearby. A Frenchwoman who had studied ballet at the Paris Opera Ballet School owned it. Though she wasn't in my ballet class, Mia took jazz and modern with me. We had so much fun. After that we began confiding in each other again, and she forgave me for treating her so poorly at school.

~

Without telling my mom or me, my ballet teacher applied to the Dance Theatre of Harlem's summer intensive on my behalf. One afternoon, as Mia and I were rushing to head off to dance class, the telephone rang. I heard my mother say to the person on the telephone, 'Yes, I'm Michaela's mother.'

'Who was it? What did they want? Was it about me? Was it my teacher? Am I in trouble?' I asked when she hung up, trying to remember if I had done anything that would require my teacher calling home.

'That was the Dance Theatre of Harlem. You've been offered a full scholarship to the summer intensive there!' my mother exclaimed.

I was overjoyed, but I also felt a little dismayed. Mia and I had grown close again, and I wasn't at all thrilled about spending seven weeks of the summer away from her.

'Can Mia apply to the summer intensive there?' I asked.

'Michaela!' my sister shouted. 'I don't want to go to ballet summer school. I'm going to jazz camp with my friends from band. Though it might not be as glamorous as an overnight programme in New York City, it's important to me. I don't want to miss it.'

'But who will talk me to sleep?' I asked, thinking of the thousands of nights that Mia either sang to me or told me stories until I fell asleep.

'You'll probably have a roommate to talk to,' Mia said, and she was more correct about that than she could have imagined.

~

When I arrived at the youth hostel where the Dance Theatre of Harlem summer intensive students stayed, I discovered that I had seven roommates and one counsellor in my room. My problem that summer was not needing someone to talk to me or tell stories at bedtime. It was having everyone quieten down so that I could sleep!

While living in the hostel, I learned that hair extensions were a very important part of the other girls' lives. I sat through many a long night as my new friends tugged and braided to give me long hair. 'That's the problem with having a white mother,' one of the girls said as she braided in my extensions.

'What is?' I asked.

'She doesn't know how to braid your hair.'

I wanted to defend my mother, but at the same time, she had never braided my hair or that of my sisters. Could it be true that white mothers couldn't braid hair? I asked myself. I felt like calling her and asking her, but worried what her answer might be. The colour of her skin had never been an issue for me. I didn't want that to change.

Besides hair extensions, the Dance Theatre of Harlem introduced me to something else that year. I had never danced in a class of predominately black dancers before that summer. Though there were many black students in the beginning levels at the Rock School, most of the students in my level were white, and we all wore pink pointe shoes and pink tights, like ballerinas the world over.

I had learned from a former teacher that wearing pink tights is supposed to give a body the illusion of greater length and extension. But pink tights don't have the same effect on a black dancer as they do on a white dancer. When I wore pink tights, I was cut in half . . . shortened, and I was already short enough. I was at a disadvantage when dancing in a room full of white ballerinas. They looked long and slim. I looked short and squat.

We were required to wear dance shoes and tights to match our skin. In the case of most of the girls, including me, that meant brown. My particular shade of brown was Fashion Brown, and it came in a spray can. I sprayed all of my pointe shoes that colour and dyed my tights the identical shade of brown. It was uplifting to be able to wear brown pointe shoes and brown tights. I had never felt so long, lean and elegant before.

~

During the summer that I danced at the Dance Theatre of Harlem, the legendary Arthur Mitchell was still the director. He was an imposing figure with a booming voice and strong presence, which made him look much taller than he really was. Though I had tremendous respect for him and eventually grew fond of him, Mr Mitchell's voice terrified me in those days. It was what my sisters and I called an African voice, and it reminded me of the voices of the authority figures in my life, like Uncle Abdullah, Papa Andrew and the terrifying debil leaders of the RUF. Though I had been in the United States for several years, I still quaked in fear of the memory of them. Whenever I heard Mr Mitchell's voice, I'd dash around a corner or into the ladies' to hide from him.

Except for his voice, everything about Mr Mitchell was wonderful. He had an incredible ability to teach. The previous spring I had gone to him with my contemporary dance routine for the Youth America Grand Prix competition. He watched it and said, 'It's pretty good, but let's make it better.' He then showed me some tiny nuances: a lift of my chin, a tilt of my shoulders, a flex of the wrist, and a brisk stomp of energy in my feet as I stepped flirtatiously in my pointe shoes. In just minutes he turned good choreography into a great dance.

During the summer intensive Mr Mitchell was always in the middle of everything. On a late afternoon in the studio, the heat might be causing everyone to droop when suddenly he would appear, and like Drosselmeyer in *The Nutcracker*, he would add a flash of magic to the room. Spines would straighten, heads would lift, and eyes would sparkle. Everyone would become instantly alert, because nothing escaped his notice. A sickled foot, a bent knee, a raised shoulder or a turned-in hip would draw his attention, and his booming voice would call out your name, causing your pulse to race. Mr Mitchell had dedicated much of his life to bringing ballet into the lives of Harlem's children, and he always managed to share his thrill and passion for ballet with his students.

Mr Mitchell nicknamed me 'Mickey D' and 'Miss Sierra Leone'. Oh, how I hated those names, but I tolerated them because I knew that he used them affectionately.

He believed that I showed promise, so he coached me privately after my regular classes ended. He even gave me a solo at the Dance Theatre of Harlem street festival. Crowds of people lined the street that day. I was so thrilled to be chosen for the solo, but I nearly fainted with embarrassment when Mr Mitchell introduced me to the crowd on the street as 'Miss Sierra Leone'.

Despite his voice, Arthur Mitchell was the first black man that I grew to trust.

Mia and my parents picked me up from the summer ballet intensive in August. On the way home my mom turned in her seat to tell me something and suddenly cried out, 'Your hair! Your head! You have bald patches!'

I panicked and began to unbraid my extensions. Mia helped me. It took us about four hours to get them out. When we got home, I washed and conditioned my hair. Then I looked in the mirror. Tears filled my eyes. I wanted braids.

The next morning I asked my mother, 'Why can't white women braid in hair extensions?'

'I don't think that has anything to do with the colour of a woman's skin, Michaela,' she answered.

'Well, can you braid in hair extensions?'

'Of course I can,' my mother answered.

'Then why didn't you ever do it before?' I asked.

'You never asked for them before.'

When Mom said that, I felt a flood of relief. There was nothing wrong with a black girl having a white mother, after all.

I gave my scalp a couple of weeks to rest, and my mother braided in hair extensions for me. They were small and fine and didn't tug at my scalp. When she was done, I had two or three hundred microbraids in my hair. It took her over twenty hours to do my entire head, but they looked like my real hair.

Soon black women began stopping me on the street. 'Where did you get these beautiful braids?' they'd ask.

'My mother did them,' I'd proudly tell them.

If she was around, I'd make a point of having them meet her. It tickled me to see the looks of astonishment on their faces when they saw that my mother was a white woman with blonde, poker-straight hair.

~

That summer ended in a burst of glory. Mia and I were intent on mending our relationship while we were on a family camping trip. All the conflicts of our sixth-grade year seemed to disappear during those magical days of kayaking on the lake and nights of toasting marshmallows by the fire. There is something so indescribably special about giggling and sharing confidences in a tent under a starry sky as Mia and I slept side by side, just as we had in the early years of our lives.

Chapter 25

The Youth America Grand Prix

When I was younger, I watched with envy when the teenagers at the Rock School participated in the Youth America Grand Prix, or YAGP. The YAGP is the largest international ballet scholarship competition in the world. I too wanted to dance a solo onstage wearing a real tutu, like the ballerina on the magazine cover that I had found years before.

In the autumn of 2005, when I was ten years old, Ms Stephanie at the Rock School finally asked me if I would like to compete in the 2006 YAGP. Of course, I jumped at the chance.

I was the first student from the Rock School to ever compete in the Pre-Competitive Division, a name that is truly an oxymoron if there ever was one, because I soon learned that this youngest division was *extremely* competitive. I wanted to do especially well so that other young dancers from the Rock School could one day compete in this division too.

One of my competition dances needed to be a contemporary one, choreographed just for me. The other dance needed to be a variation from a classical ballet. You might get away with making mistakes in the contemporary variation, even forgetting your steps, because the judges had not seen the dance before. However, you had to dance the classical variation perfectly, because all of the judges were professional dancers. They knew every step of every classical variation.

Natalya Zeiger, whom we called Ms Natasha, was my classical coach. For my classical variation Ms Natasha chose the Gamzatti variation from the wedding scene in act two of the ballet, *La Bayadère.*

I adored Ms Natasha. She had been trained at the Bolshoi Academy and danced as a soloist at the Bolshoi Ballet before coming to the United States. In my eyes, she was the epitome of a Russian ballet dancer, tall, slender, elegant and graceful. I was eager to please her.

Ms Natasha was firm but patient as she coaxed me through the steps. The version of the Gamzatti variation that I was performing was full of développés à la seconde. For each of these I had to move a leg up through the retiré position, a position in which my leg was bent and my toe was pointing to my opposite knee. Then I had to lift the leg up and unfold it to the side until my foot was high into the air and my toes pointed to the ceiling. These took a lot of concentration, control and hard work. If I did them wrong, it would just look like I was kicking my foot to the side and high into the air without any grace.

Ms Natasha was also a very kind person. She invited me to her home and spent hours teaching me how to apply stage make-up. At ten I couldn't imagine a more exciting experience than having a real ballerina teach me how to put on make-up. To this day I follow Ms Natasha's advice about eyeshadow and lipstick. I can still hear her voice telling me how to spread the light eyeshadow up to my eyebrow, and to apply the darker shade below that. 'And remember, Michaela, when you put on the eyeliner you want to go a little past the outside edge of your eye, so that your eyes look larger.'

Lipstick was a problem for me. I have very full lips, and I had to be careful not to spread my lipstick beyond their edges. Ms Natasha showed me how to use a lipstick liner before applying the lipstick, so that it was like colouring in the lines.

Ms Natasha had a whole collection of tutus that she lent her students, but they were too large for me. The YAGP doesn't require fancy or expensive costumes, and officially it states that one is not required, but I knew that all of the competitors wore beautiful costumes, and I wanted to do the same.

My mother and I spent hours online, searching for tutus to order or rent. Since this was my first ballet competition, we had no idea that tutus and custom-made costumes needed to be ordered months ahead of time . . . long before I had ever been told that I was competing. Even if time were not a factor, the prices of the tutus were too high.

'Seven hundred and fifty dollars! Nine hundred and ninety-five dollars! One thousand one hundred and fifty dollars! Oh, sweetie, we can't afford these, but maybe I can make one for you.'

'Maybe we can rent one?' I suggested.

Mom shook her head and frowned. 'It costs a hundred dollars a day to rent, and the deposit is hundreds of dollars. By the time I pay the deposit and the rental fee, especially if you make it to the finals in New York City, the cost will be nearly equal to buying one.'

'But, Mom, you'll get the deposit back when you return it,' I said, dreading the thought of wearing a homemade tutu.

'That's if you don't spill on it, rip it or lose it,' she said. I didn't think that was funny at all, but my mother was right. I was graceful in the ballet studio, but elsewhere I was always tripping and running into things. And I was constantly spilling food on my clothes.

I shrugged my shoulders and sighed. 'Okay, so how are you planning to make this tutu?'

The very next day my mother dropped me off for my ballet classes and drove to the fabric district of Philadelphia. That evening, when she picked me up, I found bags of puffy white tulle and trimming on the backseat. In one of the bags I discovered pale gold organza with iridescent gold sequined designs. 'Wow! This is beautiful!' I exclaimed.

'That's your tutu fabric. Now, I have another surprise for you,' Mom said as she passed back a smaller bag. Inside was a flat, square box. 'Open it carefully. You don't want to drop what's inside,' she warned.

When I opened the box, I let out a cry of delight. Inside lay a handcrafted, gold-plated tiara trimmed with crystals. It was perfect!

I loved the Gamzatti variation simply because it was the first variation that I did and I had nothing else to compare it to. Performing it made me feel majestic and free until the night of the competition. Then I felt jittery with worry because the Rock School had held a compulsory meeting for the YAGP participants, and I had barely enough time to get to the YAGP venue afterwards. To reach the stage in time, I had to change into my costume in the backseat of my parents' minivan. I arrived trembling about six minutes before my name was called.

This was a complicated variation, involving technically difficult and complex combinations of steps. The version that I was doing included several en dedans turns in attitude to arabesque in plié that required intense focus on my balance while I maintained a pleasant expression on my face. I also had to cross the stage in a series of développés à la seconde. How could I possibly do this in my present condition? *Breathe deeply. Relax, you're not a kid. You're Gamzatti, a Persian princess, and it's your wedding day,* I told myself as I stood in the wings.

Finally I heard the announcement: 'Michaela DePrince, age ten.' The music began, and I stepped onto the stage. I felt beautiful in my glittering tutu and tiara. For the minute and a half that the variation lasted, the difficult steps that I had agonised over as Michaela, ballet student, came easily to the glamorous Gamzatti. I lost myself in the role. It was an awesome feeling!

I won the Hope Award in Philadelphia that year. It was the top honour for dancers in my age division.

Chapter 26

A Homemade Tutu

I wasn't sure if I'd be allowed to compete at YAGP when I moved to Vermont. The director of my first ballet school in Vermont didn't believe in ballet competitions. However, after my injury caused me to change studios, I discovered that my new teacher was more than willing to help me prepare for the 2007 YAGP. She had wonderful choreography skills and used them to help me get to the YAGP in a hurry.

Again my mom sewed my contemporary costume, but it was impossible to sew a tutu on such short notice, especially since I didn't even know for sure what variation I would dance.

'May I dance the role of the dying White Swan?' I pleaded with my ballet teacher.

'Oh, Michaela, that role requires not only adult artistry, but a lifetime of heartbreak,' she answered with a gentle smile.

'Then may I do the Black Swan?' I asked.

'Michaela! The Black Swan is a seductress and you have just turned twelve.'

'Well, what's a seductress?'

Now my teacher laughed outright. 'That's why you can't be the Black Swan. You don't even know what a seductress is. Suppose you dance the role of Paquita – I think that variation number six, the jumping girl variation, would be perfect for you. You will come flying out onto the stage in a series of five grands jetés, and I know how you love that.'

Now I laughed too. The grand jeté had always been my favourite dance step. I loved leaping high and far. It gave me the sensation of taking flight! That afternoon I watched a video of my Paquita variation with my teacher, and then, after I warmed up at the barre for forty-five minutes, we worked on it for an hour and a half.

My favourite part of this variation began eight seconds into it, when I did five grands jetés, which made me feel like I was flying. Then I came down to earth, and the tough part began. Tours jetés followed. These are turns within leaps. I knew that I could lose my footing doing them if I wasn't very precise about landing. These turns were followed by arabesque into attitude turns, finishing with a double en dedans pirouette, which I found to be the hardest part. I left that first rehearsal drenched in sweat, feeling like it was midsummer. I came to my senses fast enough when I walked out into a below-zero winter snowstorm.

While I was worrying about the dance, Mom was worrying about the costume. 'Michaela, what does Paquita wear in the variation you're dancing?' she asked the next day.

'A burgundy tutu with gold trim,' I answered.

My mother's eyes grew wide with horror. 'Michaela, you'll disappear on stage!'

I laughed. She was right. Burgundy on my chocolate skin, against the navy blue background of the YAGP stage would make me disappear. I'd look like two eyes and flashing white teeth. 'Maybe we can reverse the colours,' I suggested.

Mom dashed out of the house and returned a half hour later with several boxes of fabric dye and small bottles of burgundy fabric paint. We poured the yellow dye into the bathtub and turned on the Jacuzzi to mix the dye.

We dunked the white tutu that I had worn the year before into the yellow dye and swished it around. I had no idea how heavy a wet tutu could be until I tried to lift it out. 'Mariel! Help us!' I shouted.

Mariel is probably the strongest girl I've ever met. If she wanted to, she could probably compete in weight-lifting championships, but she didn't need to lift weights that day ... just my tutu. Mariel got a grip on the bodice of the tutu and squeezed the excess water out of it. Then together we stuffed it into a plastic trash bag, giggling the whole time. Finally we carried it downstairs and dumped it into the dryer.

My once-fluffy-and-delicate tutu sounded like a bunch of tennis balls as it thumped around in the clothes dryer. I sat in the kitchen, fearing that it would turn out a tangled mess. Eventually the loud thumping stopped, replaced by a gentle swishing. When I opened the dryer, out popped a perfect golden tutu, as fluffy now as it had been before the dye job.

With my mother's help, I painted the flower petals in the lace a deep burgundy. I had a perfect Paquita tutu when we were done. I was ready for the competition.

~

It was bitter cold and snowing in Vermont when we left for the competition in Connecticut. It was a harrowing drive, and my mom tripped in the hotel, hurting her shoulder, but we made it to the event on time, where I was quickly swept up in the events of the day. I was so excited to see old friends from Philadelphia and New York City there, and make new ones from all over the East Coast.

My first variation was my contemporary, danced to exotic Middle Eastern-style music. My mother had sewn a beautiful scarlet-and-gold brocade and gauze costume, trimmed in multi-coloured crystals. My teacher had wanted me to enter the stage dancing while wearing a thin red veil draped over my face. 'Can you see through the veil?' she'd ask me over and over again during rehearsal in her brightly lit studio.

'It's perfectly okay,' I'd reassured her as I rehearsed. By the day of the competition, I knew the variation so well that I could dance it blindfolded, which turned out to be most fortunate for me.

When my music began, I dropped my veil over my face and danced onto the stage. In the darkness of the stage I couldn't see a thing! I probably should have ripped the veil from my face, because I was worried at first that I'd fall into the laps of the audience, but suddenly I got into the mood of the music, and I was no longer Michaela. I was a Bedouin dancing girl. It didn't matter that I couldn't see the stage or the audience, because I was no longer performing at the YAGP. Instead I was dancing in the sheik's tent, swaying along with the silk hangings blown by the wind.

Finally I reached the note that signalled the removal of the veil. I ripped it from my head, and the Bedouin tent disappeared. I was Michaela again. My many hours of rehearsal had paid off. I was not teetering on the edge of the stage.

When I raised my head, I saw hundreds of people

sitting mesmerised. They must have realised that I couldn't see through my veil, because at the end of the performance everyone cheered wildly. I grinned as I curtsied, and then ran off the stage.

~

After the two-day competition, I slept most of the way home, so I arrived full of energy. I was busy telling my sisters about everything when I heard my mother say to my dad, 'Would you mind driving me to the emergency room? I can't lift my arm to steer. I think that I broke my shoulder when I fell in the hotel.'

I lay awake all that night, waiting for her to get home from the hospital. The last time someone in my family went to the emergency room, he never came home. My stomach was in a tight knot by the time I finally heard the ice in our driveway crackle as our car pulled in at five o'clock in the morning. I was on the verge of tears when I heard my mother's voice in the kitchen, but I tried to play it cool when I saw her standing there with her arm in a sling.

Mom's shoulder recovered in time for her to come with me to the 2007 YAGP finals in New York City, and as soon as we got home from that event, I began thinking about my variations for the 2008 YAGP. Once again I lobbied for one from *Swan Lake*, and once again my teacher cast me as a princess. But this year I would dance the role of the ultimate teenage princess – Princess Aurora from *The Sleeping Beauty* ballet. I would dance her eighteenth-birthday variation from act one.

That year I would be in the YAGP Junior Division, and a tutu with a boned bodice was in order. Mom and I looked online for a costume. Of course, prices had gone up.

I had considered dyeing my old tutu, but Sleeping Beauty wore a rose-pink costume in act one, and if I dipped my gold tutu in pink dye, it would probably turn a weird shade of pumpkin. Besides, when I tried it on, I realised that I had grown a lot. For years Mia had towered over me. Now I was taller than her, and I couldn't even tug my tutu over my chest.

'What am I going to wear for a tutu?' I asked.

'Let me worry about the costume, Michaela. You worry about the dancing,' Mom said.

Chapter 27

My First Tour

While my mother was planning my YAGP costumes that year, Ms Madeline, a real-life fairy godmother, appeared and gave me a special gift. Madeline Cantarella Culpo is the director of the Albany Berkshire Ballet, or ABB, a small regional ballet company with studios located in Albany, New York, and Pittsfield, Massachusetts. It brings its ballets to small towns and sparsely populated areas of Massachusetts, upstate New York, Vermont and Canada, where the residents would rarely, if ever, have the opportunity to see professional ballet without the ABB.

The ABB tours *The Nutcracker* every year, using the services of a handful of professional ballet dancers, a few teenage apprentices and dozens of children from the areas it serves. The same ballet dancers and apprentices dance throughout the tour, but the children change from town to town.

When the ABB arrived in Burlington, Vermont, I auditioned for one of the child roles.

On that chilly morning in September, I arrived at the New England Ballet Conservatory, expecting to be cast as a soldier or a rat. But my teacher had other ideas in mind. She spoke to Ms Madeline about possibly taking me on as an apprentice.

After the audition, Ms Madeline took me aside and invited me to learn a variation from 'Waltz of the Flowers', one of the professional dance roles in *The Nutcracker* ballet.

I danced with all of my heart, loving every second of my role as a flower, and to my complete delight I was offered the chance to join the company on tour and even earn a small stipend. This would be my first adult role in a ballet company, and suddenly my dream of becoming a professional ballerina didn't seem out of reach.

Later I felt a little nervous. It was one thing to be away at a summer intensive with a hundred other kids. There, chaperones watched over us day and night with eagle eyes. It was quite another thing to be on tour with a dozen teens and adults in a professional company. Despite my misgivings about being away from home, I was so proud and honoured to be offered this opportunity that I didn't consider refusing.

I knew that as an apprentice with ABB, I would be able to share ballet with thousands of people throughout northern New England, and I could show the people in my small corner of the world that black girls can be ballerinas too. Many refugees from the wars in the Congo and immigrants from West Africa had been resettled in Burlington. This would be my chance to reach out to them and encourage their children to dance ballet.

I spent the next several weeks preparing for my tour. I would be missing a lot of school, but my teachers were wonderful, and instead of giving me a packet of work sheets and assignments, they handed me a list and said, 'This is the material that you'll need to cover during that time. However you do it is up to you and your parents. We trust you and them to make it happen.'

I was getting more and more nervous as my apprenticeship with the ABB approached. 'You don't need to do this, if you're not comfortable with it,' my mother told me, sensing my nervousness.

'But I really want to,' I insisted.

'You're only twelve years old, Michaela. You'll have plenty of opportunities like this in the future,' my dad said.

He might be right about that, but I had to take this chance to tour with a professional ballet troupe. It was too great an opportunity to learn. I couldn't pass it up.

When we pulled up in front of Ms Madeline's house, where I would be living, Mia exclaimed, 'Wow! Look at that beautiful haunted mansion!'

Maybe it was the look of fear on my face or maybe Mia could read my mind, but she quickly added, 'Call me on your mobile if you're afraid of ghosts at night. I'll tell you a story or sing you a song.'

As soon as we walked into the old, rambling, three-storey Victorian house we were greeted by an enormous German shepherd. Mia squeaked like a frightened mouse and ran off, abandoning me to my fate.

'Nice boy. Good boy,' I said softly, and tentatively reached my hand out to pet the dog, which was larger than me. Finally a tall girl with long, dark blonde hair came down the stairs.

'Hi, I'm Lida, and I see you've already met Ms Madeline's dog, Buddy. He won't hurt you.'

Lida was seventeen and would also be an apprentice that year. She showed me my room, which contained two beds. 'Ms Madeline sleeps in a different wing of the house, far from the rooms on this side. There's so much space up here that she said we can have separate rooms if we'd like.'

I looked at Lida and noticed that her eyes were as wide and nervous as mine. She added, 'Or we can share this room.'

'What would you prefer to do?' I asked, hoping that this older girl wouldn't object to sharing a room with a twelve-year-old.

'Share this room,' she promptly answered.

I breathed a sigh of relief. 'Me too!' I said. We both smiled at each other, relieved not to sleep alone in the old, creaky house.

She admitted, 'I think this house is haunted, so I'm thrilled to have a roommate.'

That evening after dinner, my parents departed. In the darkness of the November night, the Victorian house looked and sounded haunted. Lida and I scared ourselves into believing that every creak and groan of the old house was really a ghost prowling the halls. I dreaded getting up to go to the bathroom at night, fearful of running into a shadowy spectre in the hallway.

Lida would occasionally drive home to Albany on weekends or to a nearby friend's house to stay overnight. On those nights I'd be scared and lonely – terrified, actually – if it weren't for my new best friend, Buddy.

Though Buddy was huge and fierce-looking, I quickly learned that he had a soft heart. Whenever Lida was away, I made him stay with me in my room. Buddy kept me warm and made me feel safe from ghosts, nightmares and my fear of kidnappers, evil spirits, robbers and mice. I couldn't help but think that if Clara or Marie Stahlbaum from *The Nutcracker* had owned a dog like Buddy, the rats would not have been able to invade, and the entire plot of *The Nutcracker* would have been different.

~

During my time at Ms Madeline's, my days were filled with rehearsals. I was cast as a Mirilton (or Marzipan), performed in 'Waltz of the Flowers', the Snow and Chinese dances, and much to my surprise and pleasure, the Arabian dance! I learned that, in a small company, you danced many roles, and did whatever was needed. So I became the understudy to the men in the Trepak (or Russian) scene, which caused me to feel like a pronghorn antelope as I leaped high into the air.

The adult dancers at ABB were all very nice to me and nurturing. They took good care of me, and I felt totally safe with them throughout the entire holiday season. The men were funny. They loved to tease me about my jumping skills and often challenged me to jumping contests. I loved rehearsing Trepak, and I wished that I had an opportunity to dance it onstage. But I never did because none of the men missed a performance.

An important lesson that I learned from this experience with the ABB was that professional ballet dancers didn't have an entire term to learn one dance routine, like I had in my dance schools. The rehearsal for a ballet lasted only a few weeks, and you had to learn several dances, not just one or two, during that time. This made the experience much more intense than anything else I had experienced up until then.

The best part of that *Nutcracker* season was the actual touring. We'd travel through the snow by van from small town to small town, to picturesque opera houses decorated with holly and lights.

We worked with a different group of kids in each place, and I never got tired of seeing the happy and excited expressions on their faces when we joined them for rehearsal. To my friends back home, I was just another kid, but to these little ballet dancers, I was one of the ballet stars, and that made me feel very grown-up.

The adults in our audiences seemed just as happy to see us as the children were. They were always so appreciative. Their applause warmed my heart on those bone-chilling nights in northern New England.

My favourite role during the tour was as an Arabian. It was exotic and romantic. I was especially happy to dance it for all of my neighbours, classmates and friends in Burlington, Vermont.

The trip back home to the Burlington area was fun for me and the other apprentices. My parents provided us with lots of food, and spread out mats and duvets on our floor so that we could sleep at my house. After we left, I felt a pang of loneliness to be leaving my family again, but we had other performances ahead of us.

As much as I loved the dancing and felt so privileged

to be touring with the company, it was still hard to be away from home. One afternoon I got lost on my way back from the pharmacy to Ms Madeline's house. Another night I was convinced there was a ghost in my room. My mom talked me through my anxiety on many long phone calls, and Mia made good on her promise to sing me to sleep on the nights I was really scared.

On Christmas Eve we danced our final performance in Pittsfield. My entire family came to watch our closing night, and after the show we drove through the dark and snowy night back to our home in northern Vermont.

Chapter 28
Turning Thirteen

When I returned home from *The Nutcracker* tour, my dance teachers told me that I needed to enrol in a pre-professional ballet programme the following school year if I wanted to continue making progress. 'Where should I go?' I asked.

There were many good programmes available, but none were in Vermont, and we found only two that boarded middle school students. The closest one was in Montreal – it was three hours away from my home.

My parents drove me up to the school to audition. I was instantly accepted into the ballet school, but I would need to enrol in a private academic school that boarded ballet students my age. I was disappointed to learn that there were two problems with this plan. All of my academic subjects would be taught in French. And because I am a citizen of the United States, my parents would have had to pay a high fee for my education.

The second school was in Washington, DC, ten or eleven hours away from home. I imagined myself sick with the flu, waiting for my parents to come pick me up after shovelling ten feet of snow out of our driveway. This was not an option, so while we tried to figure out what to do about next year, I continued to work hard in my local dance classes, and I searched for a summer intensive.

We drove nearly two hundred miles over the snowy mountains to Brattleboro, Vermont, where I auditioned for a programme. I was accepted, but learned that it would cost a fortune. I didn't want my parents to pay thousands of dollars for a programme.

'Maybe I can get into one of the American Ballet Theatre summer intensives. ABT's having an audition in Boston. Can we go?' I asked.

'Sure,' my mother agreed, and she instantly registered me for the audition.

Early on the morning before my thirteenth birthday, we boarded a bus to Massachusetts. When I arrived at the tryouts at the dance studio of the Boston Ballet, I looked at the girls spilled all over the floors, stretching and warming up. I felt a sinking sensation in the pit of my stomach. It looked like I would be the only black girl auditioning.

I was shaking from nervousness when I entered, but as soon as the class began, I focused all of my energy on doing exactly what the dance instructor told us. I decided that I was going to give this my best effort and prove that a black girl could dance as well as a white girl.

Within minutes, I discovered that the audition was no different and no harder than one of my ballet classes at the Rock School had been. For the first time I understood what Ms Stephanie from the Rock School had meant by the term *muscle memory*, as my body moved automatically into position for the tendus, relevés, ronds des jambes, battements frappés, grands battements, fouettés, assemblés, arabesques, pirouettes en dedans and en dehors, grands jetés, and all of the other steps that I had grown up doing nearly every day of my life.

Towards the end of class we switched into pointe shoes. I had planned to take a well-worn and comfortable pair, but in my last class the shank of one shoe had broken. The night before I had hurriedly sewn elastic and ribbons on to a new pair and tried to break them in on the wooden floor of our family room.

Before I went to bed I had squashed them several times by closing my bedroom door on them. For good measure, this morning I had banged them against the brick fireplace. Now, when I slid my feet into them, they felt just right. As I tied my ribbons, I could almost hear Ms Stephanie reminding me to tie the knots tightly.

Much to my relief, my pointe-shoe ribbons stayed

knotted. Nothing went wrong at all in the audition, and I had even remembered to smile during class. As I left the studio, Raymond Lukens, the instructor, winked at me, and my heart soared. Maybe that was a good sign, I told myself. But by the time I had my coat on and was walking out the door, I had managed to convince myself that it was just his way of saying hello, and I probably didn't get in.

The staff told us that we'd get the results of our audition in about two weeks. I didn't know how I could possibly wait that long. Then a few days later, my mother clicked onto her email and shouted, 'Michaela! Michaela! Come here! Hurry!'

I raced into the kitchen, and she said, 'Look at this email! You've been awarded a full scholarship to the ABT summer intensive!'

'Where?' I asked, because ABT had several locations, the most prestigious of which, in the eyes of young ballerinas, is New York City.

When Mom answered, 'New York City,' I leaped around the family room, jumping over furniture and two laundry baskets, and nearly knocking myself out by running into the fireplace. But before I would leave for the summer intensive, I had so much more to do. My parents and I had agreed that if I worked really hard at my studies and finished both seventh and eighth grades in one year, I could attend the Rock School's high school programme in September . . . if I was accepted. Also I had the YAPG to prepare for.

YAGP had taken a lot of preparation that year. My teacher and I couldn't decide on what to perform for the contemporary part of the competition, so I had learned three very different dances. Each of these choices demanded something unusual from me.

One was a modern piece taught to me by the modern dance teacher in our studio. It was choreographed to a selection from 'Passion' by Peter Gabriel and required strength, flexibility and agility. At first I thought it would be easy to perform because it didn't require pointe shoes, but it was actually difficult. I felt that I couldn't understand the artistry of this piece. The modern dance felt like a gymnastic routine to me, and because I was so young and inexperienced, I couldn't figure out who or what I was supposed to be in it.

I prefer dances from story ballets that require some acting – ballets in which I can lose myself in the mind and body of another person. I also like routines that contain certain distinctive moves in the choreography. My second contemporary number was a cute and flirty dance en pointe to the song 'Partenaire Particulair'. It required acting skills and changes of facial expression. I enjoyed stomping en pointe like a pouty young woman, indecisive about her choice of boyfriend.

The third contemporary dance was the opening

variation of the wonderful ballet, *The Firebird*, choreographed by Mikhail Fokine to the music of Igor Stravinsky. *The Firebird* requires quick and nimble movements, as well as precise port de bras that imitate the flutter of a bird's wings. I spent a lot of time that year looking at birds and mimicking their movements.

My classical variation, the Princess Aurora role, was the most artistically fulfilling of my dances. I am a romantic at heart, and dancing as an enchanted young princess, whose engagement to a handsome prince is about to be announced on her birthday, thrilled me. The choreography of the ballet in this variation is stunning! I particularly loved doing the series of ronds de jambes en l'air en pointe, which begin about a minute and a quarter into the variation as I start to cross the stage. Nothing made me feel more like a real ballerina than this variation. Its demanding artistry excited me so much.

Then, as YAGP approached, I decided to experiment that year by trying my hand at choreography, rather than worrying about winning. The most exciting part about this was that I convinced Mia to do a duo ensemble piece with me. She was still taking lessons at our local dance school, though they were just for fun and exercise, because she was focusing more on her music, taking oboe, English horn, singing and piano lessons.

'But I don't really dance ballet all that well,' Mia protested when I first asked her about it.

'But it will be so much fun! I was thinking we could make it a comedy skit and dance to the music from Johnny Depp's new movie, *Pirates of the Caribbean*. You won't have to dance much. I'll hit you on the head early in the performance, and you can lie on the stage unconscious half the time. The whole idea is to travel to Torrington together and have a great time,' I said.

Mia liked that idea, and she agreed to do it. We had a blast planning our costumes. We went to a costume shop in Burlington and bought pirate costumes. Then we went to a party-supply shop and found a lightweight pirate's chest and lots of Mardi Gras bling.

We planned the skit so that we dance onto the stage as two sword-wielding pirates dressed in contrasting colours. We discover a treasure-laden chest and get into a sword fight over it. My pirate knocks Mia's pirate over the head with the flat of her sword and she collapses onto the ground. My pirate is then so elated about having the treasure to herself that she dances all over the stage, leaping over the chest and Mia's pirate. She gets so carried away that she doesn't notice that Mia's pirate has revived and carried the chest away, leaving my pirate to celebrate over nothing.

We had so much fun doing this skit. Usually we'd both start laughing so hard in the middle of it that we'd end up rolling around on the floor. Sometimes we'd argue, and each of us would have our pirates doing what we wanted them to do, so we'd often bump into each other and accidentally knock ourselves over. Once, Mia got so excited about showing the imaginary audience the bling that she forgot to get up and dance. That really had me giggling until I was breathless. I don't think I can even remember the dance steps in this routine, just the silliness and laughter.

When my mother told me not to worry about my costumes that year, she meant it. She ordered a professional tutu pattern and made me a feathered firebird tutu in red, orange and yellow, and though it was amazing, it could not compare to the splendid Princess Aurora costume.

Mom and I could not find the right fabric and lace for the Aurora costume, so we bought a used wedding gown from a local thrift store for only thirty-five dollars! I was filled with anxiety as my mother cut the ivory lace gown into pieces and dipped them in a bath of rose-pink dye. Then I watched with fascination as she sewed the pieces together to make a gorgeous tutu, nearly identical to the ones used by famous ballet companies for act one of the *Sleeping Beauty* ballet. As a final touch she sewed on thousands of tiny crystals. 'It's beautiful!' I gasped, when she presented me with the finished tutu.

I was so inspired by the combined beauty of the tutu, the choreography and the music of Tchaikovsky that I felt like I danced my personal best at the YAGP regional competition that year. Ever since then, I have longed to dance that role in a professional production of the *Sleeping Beauty* ballet.

The YAGP in Torrington, Connecticut, that year was the best experience I ever had at the competition. I won a couple of awards, and ironically I earned a score of 100 per cent from one of the judges for the modern dance that I disliked so much. But for me, the highlight was the pirate dance. Much to our astonishment, Mia and I earned an overall score of 95 per cent! High enough to qualify for the finals in New York City!

After YAGP I auditioned for the Rock School's high school programme and got accepted with a full scholarship for the dance portion of the tuition. I had spent my childhood with the teachers and the kids at the Rock School. I couldn't wait to see them in September, so I signed up to dance at the YAGP in Philadelphia that spring, thinking that I could experiment a bit more with dance.

'You can't win an award in Philadelphia,' my mother warned, 'because you've already won awards in Connecticut.'

'That's okay. It's not about winning an award,' I said. I worked on my own to learn a different classical variation and choreograph a new contemporary dance. I didn't want my mother to put any more work into costuming, so I did most of the sewing myself, figuring that if I could sew ribbons on to my pointe shoes, I could sew a couple of easy costumes.

I chose music that lent itself to draped costumes, because using a sewing machine proved to be a lot harder than I thought it would be. I kept worrying that I'd sew my fingers on to the fabric, and I almost did once.

I used a lot of paint and glue on those costumes, but my stitches and the glue held together long enough for me to perform. Both of my do-it-yourself performances scored high enough to get me to New York City, so I chose to take the contemporary from the Philadelphia competition and my Princess Aurora from the Connecticut competition to the YAGP New York finals that year.

While in Philadelphia, I had a great time seeing all of my old friends and former teachers. They made me feel like I was part of the dance school again. I hugged and cheered a lot the two days that I was there, sitting in the audience with the Rock School kids. And when I went to New York for the finals the next month, I got to hang out with them again.

Chapter 29

An ABT Summer

Before I knew it, it was summer and time to move to New York for the ABT summer intensive. Mia had decided to study American Sign Language in New York City, so that in the autumn she could work with the children in a regional deaf programme near our home in Vermont. She also enrolled in a piano intensive for teens at Hunter College and one at the Third Street Settlement Music School. It was pure serendipity that the furnished apartment that we rented had a piano sitting in the middle of the living room. The piano delighted both Mia and the elderly neighbours next door, who seemed to enjoy listening to her music.

Every morning Mia and Mom walked me to the ABT studios at Twentieth Street and Broadway, and they'd meet me there in the late afternoon to walk me home. We'd discover little shops on the way, and we loved exploring them together.

Despite the attraction of the shops, street fairs,

farmers' markets, and restaurants, my life in the city that summer revolved around ballet. I could not afford to lose focus on the reason I was there.

The competition is fierce for the world-class, top-tier companies. Ballet is probably the only career in which you begin training as a preschooler. Millions of little kids start lessons then, but as they get older and distracted by other things in life, their numbers decrease. Most ballet students drop their lessons in high school because they want a typical social life; they develop different interests that demand more of their attention; they want to be involved in sports; or because their bodies have changed. At that point they may come to the conclusion that they just were not born to be professional ballerinas. If they dance at all, they do it for exercise and pleasure. They usually take up jazz or modern, in which the criteria are more forgiving. But none of that was the case at ABT, where all of the kids were as passionate as I was.

When I stepped into the studio on my first day of class, I was stunned. I had met most of these students at the YAGP. Unlike any other class that I had ever experienced before, every student there was an excellent dancer. Each student was there to become even better and make his or her way up the ladder to a professional career in ballet. Though some of us still had some growing to do, my class at the ABT summer intensive was filled with teenagers who were very serious about ballet. They had the bodies, the talent, the competitive spirit and the drive to become professional ballerinas.

At the intensive nobody took unnecessary bathroom breaks. No one disrupted the class by clowning around. No one complained. We knew what we were there to do, and we did it. I could smell the competitiveness oozing through my classmates' pores, along with the sweat from their hard work. Yet, despite the competitiveness, no one was ever mean to another dancer in the class. No one was a prima ballerina at the age of thirteen or fourteen. The programme instilled a sense of corps de ballet in us, and expected us to be civil, courteous and humble towards each other.

I had learned many tricks in ballet. An example of this would be multiple pirouettes, sometimes eight or more, or arabesques greater than ninety degrees. These steps are not required by any classical ballet choreography in the world, but as kids we were often tempted to show off and outdo each other. I could tell immediately that ABT didn't want us to do tricks. Instead it expected us to develop the appropriate technique for our ages, control over our bodies, and artistry. So I often worked long and hard on some of the easiest steps, such as holding an arabesque at forty-five degrees when I wanted to raise my leg to ninety degrees, or doing a passé so that my toe touched my leg in precisely the right spot. These were all steps that we had learned years before, but that summer we perfected them.

I worked so hard and sweated so much in the warm studios that I wore out a pair of pointe shoes every day. Most brands of pointe shoes are made of paste, cardboard, paper and satin. Sweat makes them soggy. A pair cost more than fifty dollars, so I tried everything that I could to salvage damaged shoes. I'd line them up on the air conditioner or hang them in front of a fan until I dried the sweat out of them. Then I glued the boxes and shanks to give them extra support. I darned the tips of the boxes. If I was lucky, I could get another half day out of them.

ABT sold us tickets to their Thursday night performances at the affordable rate of twelve dollars a ticket. So when we weren't in dance class, repairing our pointe shoes or laundering the three pairs of leotards and tights that we drenched with sweat each day, we forged friendships by attending the ballet together at night. Often we'd do sleepovers, giggling into the night, but waking up early and heading off together to start another day of hard work.

My friends were from Canada, Japan, England, China, Mexico and far-flung parts of the United States. When I was younger, I had once asked a ballet teacher how she seemed to know every other ballerina in the world. That summer the answer came to me. The friends whom I made in the summer intensives were from all over the world. As we grew older and joined ballet companies, we would remember the friendships that we forged when we were young. So I felt an awareness and sense of camaraderie that I hadn't known before. I recognised that we would not only be friends and competitors now but also in the future, when we filled the ranks of the world's ballet companies.

Most of my friends left in late July, but I stayed behind to work for two weeks as an assistant teacher in the ABT Young Dancer Summer Workshop. I had the good fortune to be assigned to Franco De Vita, the principal of the Jacqueline Kennedy Onassis School at ABT. It's difficult to describe how I felt doing that. On a Friday I was a student, one of the kids training at ABT. On a Monday morning I was an adult, one of the assistant teachers.

At that point in my life I was one of the youngest children in my family. As such, I had never experienced working with younger children and worried that I might be impatient with them. I was matched up with a class of eight-year-olds, and it came as quite a surprise to me that I loved working with these young dancers. I even went back to teach the next year.

Chapter 30

My Year of Angst

Mom, Mia and I had no sooner arrived home from the most crowded area of New York State and unpacked our bags when we packed up our camping gear and headed off to the most remote part of the state, the Adirondack Mountains. We camped beside a lake, where I spent the last two weeks of the summer swimming, hiking, kayaking and watching loons with Amie, Mariel, Mia and my parents. It seemed like our days on the lake and nights around the campfire, roasting hot dogs and toasting marshmallows, were over too soon.

Almost before I knew it, we were home again and I was rushing around packing for my first term of high school at the Rock School. On the ride down to Philadelphia my head was spinning. I was in turmoil. I loved ballet with a crazy passion, but I was just beginning to recognise the sacrifices that my family made on behalf of my future. Shortly before we left I had learned that the cost of my ninth grade at the Rock School's high school programme, as well as my pointe shoes and room and board, would cost my family twice as much as their mortgage that year.

One morning a neighbour stopped by and told my parents that he had just retired. He was leaving for Florida and wanted us to keep an eye on his house. When my dad was leaving for work, I said, 'Dad, you're in your sixties. When are you going to retire?'

He laughed.

'Mom, why did you adopt so many children?' I asked.

'Which of you should we have left behind in an orphanage? You?' Mom asked.

That thought sent chills up and down my spine. 'Maybe . . . maybe I should stop taking ballet lessons so Dad can retire,' I said, unsure of what my mother's answer would be.

'Isn't that your passion . . . your dream?' she asked.

'Of course,' I answered.

'Then you focus on your dancing. We'll retire someday, but certainly not now.'

As we neared Philadelphia I thought of the sacrifices that I had made too, so that I could become a ballerina. As a child I loved ballet so much that I had even turned down birthday party invitations so as not to miss classes. I had given up swimming, and public school. And now it seemed that I was giving up the time I could be spending with my family.

I asked myself, suppose I wake up someday and decide that I hate ballet? Would I regret the sacrifices that I had made? As hard as I tried to imagine such a day, I couldn't. I felt that ballet was in my bones and in my blood. It was all wound up with who I was. I would give up breathing air before I would give up ballet.

When we pulled up in front of the Rock School, I was full of optimism and floating on a cloud. I was certain that it would be like living in paradise and I'd have a perfect year. But as soon as my parents helped me unload and said their goodbyes, my feet touched the ground. By the next morning I was miserable. We had been assigned roommates by age, so my close friend Ashley had been given a different roommate. I didn't know my new roommate, and though we'd eventually become friends, at that time we didn't know each other. Whom could I talk to late at night when I was feeling insecure?

To make matters worse, one of the adults in our dorm reminded me of Auntie Fatmata, so that's how I referred to her in my mind. I was convinced that she hated me. This made me homesick and I felt like Number Twenty-Seven again.

It took me a couple of months to learn that most of the other girls thought that 'Auntie Fatmata' hated them too. She would give us detention and ground us for a month for even slight infractions. I was thirteen and rather rebellious at that age, so there were times when I definitely broke rules. I expected to be punished for that, but as soon as I learned the rules, 'Auntie Fatmata' made new ones, which she'd often fail to tell us about until we broke them. I remember getting a month of grounding for eating a granola bar in the lounge and another month of grounding for sharing my muffin with another student. To me the only good thing about those groundings was that we had to spend them studying, so I was way ahead in my schoolwork, and my grades were great as a result of all that punishment.

I was one of the youngest kids in the high school programme. Except for my early years in Africa, I had been sheltered by my parents throughout my life. Now I was around older teens day and night. Some of them took me under their wings. What they taught me would make my parents' hair stand on end, but at that time I really believed that these older kids knew everything.

That year I learned from an older student that alcohol mixed with a power drink would relax my muscles, relieve the stress of 'Auntie Fatmata', and ease the pain of tendonitis. Someone suggested I try it once when I was off campus. I did and never tried again because it made me violently ill.

One of the older girls recommended an all-tea diet to lose weight. I tried that for one day, and shook so badly that I could barely stand en pointe. I thought I had some terrible disease and called my mother for medical advice.

Someone else told me that smoking cigarettes would help me relax as well, and they had the added benefit of helping me lose weight. But, like tea, cigarettes made me shake. They also gave me a sore throat and asthma, neither of which helped me relax.

One girl recommended skipping meals, taking laxatives and vomiting after meals in order to keep thin. I'd often watch her cut her food into tiny pieces and spread it all over her plate to make it look like she had eaten. When I was little, I had experienced starvation and dysentery. I knew what it was like to starve or vomit until you were nearly dead, and I decided not to control my weight in any of those ways.

My father worked in New Jersey, so he visited me once a week. On one of his visits he sighed and said, 'Michaela, I know you'll find this hard to believe, but there's a reason for the minimum age for smoking and drinking.' I felt so contrite when I saw the disappointment in his eyes.

My favourite saying had always been, 'To thine own self be true.' Being true to myself meant throwing myself into my ballet, and not letting anything get in the way of my goals.

I had been placed in the highest-level ballet class at the Rock School. I felt that I needed to prove to myself that I really belonged there. The auditions for the Rock School's *Nutcracker* were coming up. I worked hard preparing for it. I wanted to dance flawlessly during the audition so that I would get a choice role.

'Don't be disappointed if that doesn't happen,' Mia warned me during one of my telephone calls home. 'You're only a freshman. The Sugar Plums will probably fall to the older girls.'

On the day of the auditions it was clear to me that older and taller girls would be cast as the Snow Queen, the Sugar Plum Fairy, and Arabian. Children in classes lower in level than mine would be cast as Clara, Party Children, Soldiers and Pollys. I suspected that I'd be a flower in 'Waltz of the Flowers', or a Snowflake in the snow scene. Smile. Look happy. *Dance your very best,* I told myself on the day of the audition. *You'll have more opportunities in the future.*

When the cast list was posted, I saw that I had been given the role of Dewdrop. I was most familiar with the Balanchine *Nutcracker* from having watched the video practically every day with Mia as a kid. In that ballet Dewdrop is the lead character in 'Waltz of the Flowers', and tiptoes among the flowers as she dances her solo. Since she is only a tiny dewdrop fairy on the petals of the flowers, she is supposed to be small and delicate. My greatest desire as a ballerina was to be delicate, so I was very grateful to be given this dainty but challenging role.

When rehearsals began, I was shocked to discover

that in the Rock School's *Nutcracker*, Dewdrop dances among the other characters throughout most of the ballet and has two rather long solos. It was going to be intense to learn all of Dewdrop's moves with two separate casts, while at the same time I was learning a classical variation, from *La Esmeralda*, and a contemporary dance for the Philadelphia YAGP 2009 in early January. But I loved a challenge.

My parents drove down from Vermont to see me perform in *The Nutcracker*. My mom later told me, 'As we waited in the audience during intermission, Ms Stephanie came rushing over to tell us that you were injured. You might not dance the second act. We were crushed, but we said that with the YAGP coming up, you needed to care for yourself.'

Even Ms Stephanie didn't know that I would dance until I entered the stage smiling. My ankle was painful and tender, but I didn't let it show on my face. I would never allow the audience to see how I was feeling. Even at thirteen I believed that the audience should think that the hardest combination of steps is effortless, and a ballerina's personal trials and tribulations shouldn't show on her face. So I was overjoyed to dance the second act flawlessly, looking as though I didn't have a care in the world. After the show I was able to moan and groan to my heart's content as I iced my ankle and then hobbled off to greet my parents.

I recovered at home on my half-term break and returned two weeks later, ready to compete in the YAGP. I had always wanted to dance *La Esmeralda* in competition, even though this variation, danced with a tambourine in hand, begs for criticism. Ms Natasha, who was my competition coach once more, warned, 'The tambourine is not just a prop. It's a part of your dance. If you don't use it artistically, the judges will tear you apart!'

Of all the classical dances approved for use in YAGP, performing *La Esmeralda* might be the most difficult because of the staccato beat of the music. When I was dancing this variation, it was tempting to move my body stiffly to accompany the staccato, but this would have made me look jerky, like a marionette.

Esmeralda is a poor Gypsy girl who is in love. When I danced as her, I focused on making my body and limbs move smoothly. I made an effort to flirt with the audience so my character would seem more relatable and less mechanical.

On the day of the competition I did my best. I knew that I had dropped my heel during a pirouette, and though I had danced for the crowd and the audience loved it, I wasn't convinced that the judges loved it. That's why I was totally blown away when I was awarded the Youth Grand Prix, the top award for my age division.

Chapter 31

First Position

In the autumn of my freshman year of high school, I received a letter from ABT, informing me that I had been named a National Training Scholar. This meant that I had received a full scholarship to the 2009 ABT summer intensive in New York City. This scholarship covered both my tuition and my board. That year the summer intensive students would be staying at a college dormitory, so when I was fourteen, I spent the summer of 2009 in the city without my mother and sister.

While I was away, my family had moved into a house across the street from the high school that my sisters would attend. It was a larger house, and their timing was perfect. Though Amie, now an adult, had moved out on her own, our family grew by two more children that summer.

Bernice and Jestina, both nine years old, were the adopted daughters of my brother Adam and his wife, Melissa. Before their adoption in 2003, these two little girls had been living in a Liberian orphanage. It was one of the poorest and most unsupervised in the world. Chaos reigned in their orphanage of two hundred and ninety-five children and one caregiver.

They had come to Adam and Melissa almost like feral children.

With no other experience raising children and with no formal training in child development, Adam and Melissa were at their wits' ends with the girls. When Adam and Melissa separated, the care and upbringing of Bernice and Jestina proved to be overwhelming, so my parents accepted guardianship of the girls.

When I came home from the ABT summer intensive, I struggled to catch up with the American Sign Language, or ASL, that the family used with Bernice, who was deaf. Unlike Mia and Mariel, I had no talent for ASL, but Bernice and I bonded when I taught her ballet, hooking up the stereo on the deck so that the wooden floor reverberated with the beats. Bernice had such a natural ability for ballet that it nearly broke my heart that her deafness prevented her from studying it professionally.

One of the problems of teaching deaf students was that the music needed to be played very loud in order for them to feel it. Few dance schools could do that. The volume could injure the other students and teachers.

I would have loved to teach her all year round, but the summer was drawing to a close and I'd soon have to return to Philadelphia. However, my experience with Bernice convinced me to include deaf students someday when I owned my own studio.

Over the summer I learned that 'Auntie Fatmata' wasn't returning. I was vastly relieved about that but torn about going back to Philadelphia. Living apart from my family was painful to me. I would never have done it for anything other than ballet.

I was thinking about all of this when my mother popped her head into the doorway. She told me that she had received an email from a woman named Bess Kargman, who was producing a ballet documentary.

'She asked if you'd want to participate,' my mother said.

'Do you trust her?' I asked.

'Yes, she comes recommended by the YAGP. She received approval from them to follow some of the kids who competed, if the parents give their permission,' Mom explained.

Thinking that it involved only a brief interview, I agreed. Once I was back at school, Bess began to come around with her camera and crew. At that time I was very shy about being videotaped, and Bess wanted to videotape me doing everything. She would follow me around, taping my meals, my dance classes and my rehearsals. She followed me home to interview my parents and siblings. She even followed me backstage during competitions. Sometimes when she'd come, I'd hide in my closet, hoping that she'd leave if she couldn't find me.

'Michaela, you've always talked about wanting to make the world aware that black girls can be ballerinas too. Maybe Bess's documentary will help you accomplish that,' my mother said.

I gave some serious thought to that and decided to make myself more available to Bess. Even with a purpose in mind, I still found it difficult to participate in the filming of *First Position*.

~

In the orphanage I had learned to be stoic and hide my true feelings, so I was not used to expressing myself openly. When Bess arrived, she wanted me to share my feelings. She could see right through insincerity. She asked hard questions and demanded honesty. This was especially true when she asked me about my wartime experiences in Sierra Leone and my life in the orphanage.

The few memories I had of my early years were painful ones. Just thinking of the debils and the dead bodies that littered the streets of my homeland gave me nightmares. Many times I was reduced to tears during the filming. After an interview I would have difficulty sleeping for days.

During one interview I told her my birth name. When I realised what I had done, I became very upset. I worried about that for months afterward. Because *Bangura* is the most common name in Sierra Leone, I worried that some unrelated person with that name would claim to be my parent and take me away from my American family.

Bess's prying camera caught me during moments of joy, like when I greeted my parents after my successful performance in the 2010 YAGP in Philadelphia, and times of contentment, like when I picnicked with my family on the deck of our home during an unseasonably warm spring day. It caught me during moments of despair as I suffered from a painful case of tendonitis during the YAGP New York finals. Before I stepped onto a stage, I needed time to centre myself and concentrate on what I would do, but Bess was right there with her camera. *Remember, you can reach out to people and let them know that black girls can be ballerinas too,* I'd ultimately remind myself whenever I felt uncomfortable under the eye of the camera.

While I was emoting for Bess, I was also looking inward and beginning to analyse who I was. I decided that I didn't particularly like the grumpy, pushy, selfish girl who would sometimes appear, especially because those aspects of my personality interfered with my dancing. I was striving for a dance style that was strong yet soft, delicate and gracious. When Bess was filming me, I was fourteen and already able to dance with excellent technique, great strength and agility, but the gentle, soft, delicate and gracious part was still missing.

I knew that I needed to change the way I acted if I wanted to achieve my goals in ballet, but I had no idea how to bring all that together. In the Rock School studios, Ms Stephanie struggled patiently and endlessly with me to bring out the soft side of my dancing and personality, but I felt that I still had not achieved enough of it by the time I was fifteen years old.

At the 2010 YAGP I was awarded a full year-round scholarship to the Jacqueline Kennedy Onassis School, or JKO, at ABT. Bess recorded that moment in *First Position*, and I am glowing in that scene. This scholarship would cover everything: room, board, food costs . . . It lifted a heavy burden from my family.

Yet, when people discuss *First Position* with me, I learn from them that it isn't the happy glow of my face that they remember.

I had been distraught when Bess videotaped me, sitting with my foot packed in ice, shortly before I had to perform in a dance competition, and it is this image that many people take away with them. This image lets the world know that injuries and pain are facts of life for us. It symbolises all the sacrifices that ballerinas make for their art.

Many people who saw Bess's documentary ask me how I was injured and why I continued to dance that day. I tell them that those beautiful satin pointe shoes that I had longed for since age four are not sturdy footwear. It's common for a ballerina to come down from a leap, or out of a turn, and twist an ankle or pull a tendon. My weakest spot was my Achilles tendon. In *First Position*, I faced the possibility of being eliminated from YAGP because of my injury. The decision was mine – totally. I asked myself, *Should I dance or should I sit it out?*

My teachers recommended that I sit it out. They were concerned about any long-term effects of dancing on an injured foot. I was only concerned with winning a scholarship to a school that every dancer aspired to attend – a school that would guide me to my ultimate dream.

That day I squeezed my swollen foot into my pointe shoe and pretended that my tendon didn't hurt. I danced onto the stage and did a variation that required many grands jetés. When people ask me how I did that, I honestly don't know. I think that when I stepped onto the stage and heard the roar of the audience, I had such a rush of adrenaline and joy that I didn't notice the pain.

Chapter 32

Growing Up

Somewhere between the ages of fifteen and eighteen, I grew up, both as a human being and as a dancer. It didn't happen all at once. I attended the ABT programmes, the summer intensive and JKO, year-round. The first year was bumpy for me. It had its ups and downs, emotionally, physically and artistically. I found it so difficult to express the artistry and emotion that I needed for my roles. This frustrated not only me, but some of my teachers as well. Sometimes I wanted to burst into tears in class because I sensed their disappointment.

I was always a very down-to-earth person. If I felt stormy, I showed it on my face when I was supposed to look serene. Acting came hard to me, and ballerinas need to be actresses as well as dancers onstage. But as I grew from a young teen to a young woman, I finally gained the artistry that had been lacking in my dancing. I also acquired the graciousness that had eluded me at thirteen, and made it a part of my dancing and my daily life.

When I was younger, I had tried to act grown-up by hiding my thoughts, feelings and behaviour from my parents. I had thought that this was a sign of adulthood. Ironically, I discovered that as I grew older, I became more open with my parents. At the age of thirteen I went to my friends for advice, but the advice that they gave me usually wasn't very good. But at the age of eighteen I went to my parents. I discovered that they gave much better advice, especially about health, money and many of the other complicated issues related to the world of adults, which I was then facing.

Fortunately, my family was able to move to New York City when I was sixteen. When I turned seventeen and got a job in a professional ballet company in New York City, I was finally able to move into an apartment with a friend. But I surprised myself by choosing to continue to live with my family for another year.

I've often heard it said that professional ballerinas neglect their education in order to achieve their goals as dancers. There was no way I would do that. My family values education too much. My father would often say, 'Suppose a taxicab runs you over tomorrow, and you can never dance again. What would you do without an education?'

Such a gruesome possibility! I didn't want to think of something like that happening, but my dad forced me to, so I worked hard in school. I attended an excellent accredited online high school for four years. Often, friends who attended private or public schools would comment on how lucky I was . . . how easy it was for me to do my schoolwork whenever it was convenient for me. I laughed at that. Every course in my school came with a thick, heavy textbook. Unlike regular high schools, where the teachers often skip over some pages or chapters, my high school required its students to read every word on every page of every textbook, and the tests were designed to make sure that we did. Every section of every chapter was accompanied by a quiz and essay questions.

How I dreaded those essay questions! I wrote at least two hundred essays every term. I hated those essays so much that I even took maths by choice, just to avoid them. Then I discovered that my maths course included a major research paper that required tons of writing. When I finally graduated with honours in 2012, I felt proud of that accomplishment, and relieved that I no longer had to face those five-paragraph essays late at night after dancing all day.

I was a typical kid in many ways. When I was thirteen, I spent most of my winter holiday crying about a boy who said he liked me one day and would change his mind the next. Once I asked my mother, 'How will I know if a boy loves me?'

She said, 'He'll be your friend. He'll make you happy.

He'll give you space and remain faithful to you. He'll respect your choices. He'll let you soar and not try to clip your wings.' Then she concluded with a smile, 'And he wouldn't dream of making you cry through the holidays.' When I was almost seventeen, despite my many hours in the dance studio and my nights at home with my schoolbooks, I managed to find time to fall in love. I was lucky enough to fall in love with a young man who was capable of doing all the things my mother had described to me. His name is Skyler; he's a ballet dancer and choreographer. Skyler understands how important ballet is to me and remains faithful to me when I travel the world. We share dreams for the future. One of them is to someday dance with the same company and be cast as partners in pas de deux.

It was fortunate for me that I had matured emotionally when I did. Without that newfound maturity, I probably could not have handled all of the changes that took place in my life after *First Position* was released in September 2011.

Chapter 33

After First Position

In August 2011, *First Position* was accepted into the Toronto Film Festival. Bess arranged for Mia and me to see it before its premiere at the festival. Tears poured down my face as I watched it for the first time. I wasn't crying over the telling of my story, recalling the pain of dancing through my injury, or the award of a scholarship. I was crying because I was overwhelmed by emotion for what I sensed the film had unleashed. I knew that my life was about to change in a way that I could not predict. And that scared me. I was a very private person. I had opened up to Bess, but I knew that others would expect this of me.

In addition to the Toronto Film Festival, Bess was invited to enter *First Position* in other film festivals, and her film was nominated for several prestigious awards, including the NAACP Image Award. It gained the attention of the whole world. Soon everyone was watching it, including producers of television programmes, the news media, and artistic directors of ballet companies.

As the film's fame flourished, interest in me as a person and a ballet dancer grew.

Suddenly newspapers, magazines and television programmes contacted me. I wondered what I should do. I could either hide from them, or accept their invitations. I had always wanted to be a role model to little girls and an activist for change. Here was my opportunity, staring me in the face.

As a result of *First Position*, I had the good fortune to be featured in quality magazines like *Marie Claire* and *Teen Vogue*. Next, invitations from television programmes came pouring in. I was interviewed for ABC's *Good Morning America* and *Nightline*, and in April 2012 I was invited to be the AT&T Spotlight guest on *Dancing with the Stars* and was flown to Los Angeles with my mom. Soon I managed to control my shyness and enjoy these wonderful experiences.

As exciting as some of these were, my first focus was still my dancing, so to me the most wonderful outcome of the attention I received from *First Position* was an invitation by Dirk Badenhorst, the CEO of the South African Mzansi Ballet.

Mr Badenhorst had seen *First Position* and requested permission to watch me during my class at JKO. Initially, all I knew of his plan was what the JKO principal told me: 'Dirk Badenhorst, from South Africa, will be in the class to observe you.'

When I learned after class that Mr Badenhorst wanted me to dance a principal role in *Le Corsaire* as a guest of his company, you could have knocked me over with a feather. I immediately telephoned my mother from the dressing room, but I was so excited I didn't realise that she couldn't make any sense of what I was saying. When I finally got home, my family was shocked that I was going to South Africa on my own.

Later that night my mother came to me with a bulging file folder. It was labelled AFRICAN ADOPTION. She said, 'I was planning to give these to you when you turned eighteen, but if you're going to Africa, I think that you should be aware of what is in them.' Then she showed me a series of articles about a group of children from Sierra Leone whose alleged parents had come forward, claiming that their children had been stolen from them during the war. They said that their children were trafficked to the United States and sold to white Americans.

Mia, Mariel and I were on the list of children. I began to protest. 'This isn't true,' I insisted. This man who's claiming to be Mia's father . . . he can't be. She told me every night that she had seen her father run down by a lorry full of laughing debils. Then I began to tremble, fearing that I'd find that Uncle Abdullah was trying to reclaim me.

I continued reading, and when I saw that a woman

with the last name of Bangura was listed as my mother, I became indignant. 'The name of this woman who is claiming to be my mother . . . well, that's not my mother's name. I had my father's last name, but my mother's last name was different. And I saw my mother's dead body, I . . .' I began to cry, not as much from sorrow as from anger and frustration that people should come forward now, when we were nearly full-grown, and insist that we return to a world we didn't know.

'Yes, you're probably correct about your parents,' my mother agreed. 'Papa Andrew told me that both of your parents had died, and you had remained with your mother till the end.'

Then she asked all three of us, 'Do you want to pursue this further? Dad and I are willing to help you, if you want to contact these people who claim to be your parents. I want you to give it a lot of thought. Here, take this file, then talk about it among yourselves and sleep on it.' Even though the woman who claimed Mariel was really her biological mother, Mariel refused to discuss it with us that night. 'I'm perfectly happy being Mariel DePrince,' she announced, and then she rolled over and fell asleep.

Mia and I stayed awake late, talking about Sierra Leone and the articles Mom gave us. We realised that once we were out of Africa and in the heart of a loving family, that country and all of the sorrow we had experienced had eventually ceased to exist in our minds. However, since the release of *First Position*, the media had brought it up so frequently that we had to address it.

There were many articles that criticised the way our adoptions had been handled. The adoptions were described as 'human trafficking' and worse. In an online blog an American activist said that we might have been better off with our birth parents. This angered me. We had hidden behind trees to avoid being shot by debils. We had arrived here so sick that it's likely that we would have died if we remained in Africa much longer. I needed abdominal surgery within weeks of my arrival. Mia and I truly believed that our adoptions had been lifesaving.

What did bring tears to our eyes that night were the notes our mother had taken when we told her about our lives in Africa as little orphan pikins.

'This is so sad,' Mia cried loudly.

'Oh, these poor little girls. What a sad story!' I said, wiping my tears and sniffing.

Mia's eyes grew round, and she laughed through her tears. 'Michaela, we are these little girls!'

I laughed and cried at the same time. 'Weren't we so pathetic back then? Our lives were so hard; we were so sick all the time. But I barely remember this. When I think of being a little girl, I remember Daddy taking us to *The Nutcracker* and Mom baking holiday cookies with us.'

'And campfires. And Teddy throwing us into the air and swinging us around the playroom,' Mia said.

'And taking us to the movies and the park, and trick-or-treating,' I added.

'Remember the time . . .'

Before we knew it, we were reminiscing about Teddy and our childhood in America. Laughing and crying over memories that had accumulated over thirteen of the seventeen years of our lives, I realised that we had gone off track. 'Mia, we're supposed to be talking about reconnecting with Sierra Leone; instead we're talking about our family.'

Mia opened her eyes wide. 'Okay, did you hear what you just said?' she asked.

I looked at her with a sheepish grin. 'Yeah, our family . . . I got it.'

When we returned to the topic of Sierra Leone, our discussion centred on what we could do for the people there, especially the women and children. The boys and girls, but especially the girls, lacked opportunities for education. Education wasn't free, and families couldn't afford the hefty school fees. Three-quarters of the women couldn't read and write. One out of eight women died in childbirth. More than 90 per cent of girls in Sierra Leone endured female genital mutilation.

Recently laws were passed criminalising rape and domestic violence, but the country lacked the funds to enforce the laws.

'So what will your answer be?' Mia asked. 'Remember; Mom asked, "Do you want to pursue contact with the people claiming to be your family members?"'

'No, I'm not interested in finding biological relatives. I'm Michaela DePrince now, and that's who I've been for a long time. But when I'm older, I'd like to start a free art school in Sierra Leone, and teach ballet there.'

'I can help you. I'll bring over a pile of instruments and teach music,' Mia offered. 'But I'm not ready to return now . . . maybe in twenty years.'

'Me too,' I murmured. 'In the meantime we can figure out a way to raise money for education in Sierra Leone.'

Even though I had come to terms with who I was and the role Africa had played in my life, on the day before my departure for South Africa, I awoke in the predawn hours, sweating and shivering with fear. My dreams had been filled with dreadful memories of Africa. It had been the first time in years that the terrors of my early childhood had come back so vividly to haunt me. This made me wonder if I was ready to return.

More than anything else, I feared being kidnapped and returned to the home of Uncle Abdullah. I got out my computer and did a Web search. I discovered that it was a five-hour flight from Johannesburg, South Africa, to Freetown, Sierra Leone. I pulled out the huge atlas that our oldest brother had given to us. I was reassured to see that Kenema District, where I had been born, was two-thirds of a continent away from Johannesburg, a distance of over five thousand miles.

When I shared my worries with Mia, she said, 'I'd estimate that it would take at least ten days for someone to drive that distance. I don't think it's worth anybody's time or trouble to kidnap you.'

Chapter 34

Returning to Africa

Despite my sister's reassurances, I was jittery and nervous at four-thirty in the morning, the time I left for the airport. I hadn't even got on my plane when I called my mother to tell her that I missed her.

'Already!' She laughed. Then her voice grew serious, and she asked, 'Are you feeling okay?'

'I'm just a little scared, you know ... of going to Africa.'

'You'll be fine. Dirk Badenhorst told me that he and his company would take good care of you.'

I usually fall asleep easily in any vehicle with a humming motor, but I was too nervous and afraid to sleep at all during the twenty-hour trip to South Africa. My knees shook as we took off, and they continued to shake until I saw the smiling face of Mr Badenhorst when we landed.

~

I could not believe how welcomed Mr Badenhorst's ballet company made me feel. It was a lovely classical company with caring and friendly directors and dancers. I would have loved to work with them full-time, but the trip to South Africa from my parents' home was far too long. My parents were in their sixties at the time, and I knew that the trip to visit me there would not only be expensive but physically hard on them too. Besides, I loved my adopted country, and I longed to dance where I could return to it frequently.

There was a group of dancers from Cuba there too, and they tried to convince me to come to Cuba and dance with the Cuban National Ballet. *Cuba isn't so far from the United States,* I decided, but then I remembered the political situation and realised that despite the allure of that beautiful company, joining them would be impossible for me. So I had to enjoy the experience of performing with these wonderful dancers while we were all far from our respective homes.

~

Until now I had only danced in two full-scale ballets. One was *The Nutcracker*, of course, and the other was *Abdallah and the Gazelle of Basra*, in which I had danced as a guest of De Dutch Don't Dance Division in the Hague, Netherlands, while a JKO student.

The South African Mzansi Ballet's production of *Le Corsaire* would be my debut performance as a professional ballerina. I had always expected that my debut as a professional would be as part of a corps, so I was bedazzled to be dancing the role of the slave girl, Gulnare, partnered with Andile Ndlovu, a South African dancer.

I had wanted to spend all of my time in South Africa perfecting my role. I had danced some of the variations of the other female lead, Medora, but I had never danced the Gulnare variations and the pas de deux. I felt that it would require all of my attention, but I quickly learned that, in South Africa, ballet was big news and ballerinas were almost like rock stars! So immediately I was whisked off to a television interview.

My time in South Africa was filled with frenetic energy and frantic activity. I was scheduled for interviews, speaking engagements, lots of rehearsals, costume fittings and of course the performances. I had arrived on the seventh of July, and *Le Corsaire* opened twelve days later! I had never learned anything that quickly before! I loved every second of it, though I must admit that at times I became very tired. During one televised interview, I felt my eyelids drooping and I prayed that I wouldn't fall asleep in my chair.

Before I left for South Africa, my father had warned me that Johannesburg could get very cold in the winter.

When I asked Andile about that, he said, 'Oh no, the winters are very mild, even in Joburg.'

On the day I departed, my mother tried to shove extra sweat suits into my luggage, and I had protested, worried that I wouldn't be able to lift the bag. During my visit, Joburg experienced a cold snap and one of its rare snowfalls. This delighted the residents of South Africa, but I froze.

The weather might have been too cold. The schedule might have been too crazy. But the experience of the ballet was worth everything. Mundane worries that I had during rehearsals, like being dropped during a high lift or twisting an ankle in a turn or, horror of horrors, forgetting the choreography – these all disappeared when I stepped from behind the curtain and into the life of Gulnare.

My entire experience there was enlightening. The prima ballerina in the company taught me by example that it was possible to be on top and still remain genuine and generous. I learned from the very kind director that there was no need for someone in his position to remain aloof and haughty as others often do. And the children of South Africa taught me something about myself.

The US embassy had invited me to give a motivational talk in a school. At first I was scared to do this. I was remembering my middle school years and all of the chatting that went on in the classrooms. I don't have a strong voice, and I worried that I wouldn't be heard over the noise of the students' voices.

When I entered the school and was escorted to the class where I would give my talk, my knees knocked together. *This is really traumatic,* I thought as I took a deep breath, and opened my mouth to introduce myself. Suddenly silence fell on the room. Not a voice could be heard other than mine. All eyes were upon me.

The rapt attention of the students gave me courage, and I began to tell my story. As I spoke to them, much to my surprise, I discovered that I was actually far better at this than I thought I would be. These courteous and dignified students probably motivated me far more than I motivated them that day. With my confidence buoyed, I realised that a ballerina could do more than dance.

After *First Position* was released in 2011, people on the streets began to notice me. They'd come up and ask, 'Are you Michaela DePrince?' At first I dreaded this attention. I felt too shy to respond with anything other than a quiet, mouselike hello. After I returned from speaking to those kids in South Africa, I found my voice. Now I look at every encounter as a means of touching a life.

Chapter 35

Finding a Company

The trip to South Africa had revived my flagging spirits. In the spring my self-esteem had taken a battering. I had worked so hard that year. I had not only danced from morning till night in both Level 7 at JKO and with the ABT Studio Company, but I had completed high school while doing both. Then Franco De Vita told me that I would not be dancing in the studio company the following year. He said that I was ready to audition for a professional company. That day, when I arrived home, late as usual and exhausted from many hours of dancing, I burst into tears. My heart was broken, my dreams dashed.

I had expected to spend another year in training with the studio company. But here I was, cut loose at seventeen, my dream of joining ABT's professional company shattered. Instead of languishing in my misery, I picked up my broken heart and began auditioning for North American classical ballet companies.

One company told me that at five feet, four and a

half inches tall, I was too short, and eliminated me immediately. I travelled over a thousand miles to another audition, only to be refused admission. That company told me that it hadn't received my resume and head shot, yet I had confirmed their receipt of both before flying there. I auditioned for other companies, and was always one of five or six dancers remaining at the end of each audition. Yet I wasn't hired by any of them.

Of course, I had known since I was eight years old that classical ballet companies were predominantly Caucasian. That probably isn't even the most accurate way to describe the major classical ballet companies. Now, in my anger and frustration, I could find no nice words to describe their lack of black female dancers.

Nine years before, I had searched eagerly for a black female face among the white ones and hoped that, with time, attitudes would change and more would appear. When I looked again, there were fewer black ballerinas. Lauren Anderson had since retired from the Houston Ballet, and a few other black women had given up their battles of trying to make it in a classical company. No one had replaced them.

During those dark days, I met Alonzo King when his famous contemporary company, Alonzo King Lines Ballet, performed in New York City. He invited me to take a company class with Lines, and afterwards he asked me about my dream for the future.

I admitted to him that my dream had always been to dance with a classical company. He understood this and respected my dream, but he also told me that if I someday grew tired of classical ballet, I was welcome to join his company. I was honoured as much by the fact that he understood that I needed to be true to myself as I was by his invitation.

It came as no surprise to me that the only companies that welcomed me were Alonzo King's Lines and the Dance Theatre of Harlem's new professional company. Both were predominantly ethnic, and neither of them were classical companies. They were both wonderful companies. I would feel proud to dance with them, but I knew that my heart wouldn't belong to either of them, at least not now, when I longed to dance with a classical company.

The Dance Theatre of Harlem, or DTH, was a neo-classical company, heavily influenced by George Balanchine. Arthur Mitchell, the first black dancer to perform with the New York City Ballet, and Karel Shook, a white dancer and ballet master, believed that there should be a place for black dancers in the art of ballet. So they founded DTH.

From 1969 until 2004, DTH travelled the world, performing to great acclaim. Then, under the pressure of tremendous debt, it closed its doors, keeping only its school and ensemble open in order to provide ballet training to the black children of Harlem and beyond, preparing them for careers that, sadly, were almost non-existent.

DTH had forty dancers, and it was able to perform full-scale ballets in its heyday. Now, after heroic fundraising by its board of directors and several major corporate donations, DTH's professional company was about to return, but with only eighteen dancers.

I auditioned for it. I was accepted, and I was most grateful for the opportunity extended to me by Virginia Johnson, its former principal dancer and now its new artistic director. I wanted to contribute to the company's return to the world of professional ballet. I wanted to be a part of its return to former glory. However, I knew deep down inside that my heart belonged elsewhere.

DTH sent me a letter of intent that needed to be signed by the twenty-sixth of April. Once I signed it, I'd be committed to DTH for the 2012–2013 ballet season. I agonised over that decision. Because of my experience with Arthur Mitchell, I felt affection for DTH, but was that enough? As I stared at that letter of intent, I felt like Juliet, agreeing to marry her cousin Paris while longing for Romeo. DTH, like Paris, deserved more than affection. It deserved the love that I couldn't give it.

I decided to spend a year with it. The experience would be invaluable to me, and hopefully some of the media attention I was getting would benefit DTH. If, at the end of that year, my soul wasn't satisfied by the company's repertoire and I didn't feel passionate about it, then I could audition elsewhere.

If the US didn't want me, perhaps Europe would, I told myself. I knew that I needed to be eighteen to qualify for a European Union work visa. I decided that once I turned eighteen, I could seek work with the classical companies of Europe.

Finally I signed the DTH letter of intent and faxed it exactly on the deadline. A few days later Franco De Vita invited me to officially join the ABT Studio Company, and two months later ABT offered me the position of company apprentice. As an apprentice, I would learn its repertoire and perform in its production of *The Nutcracker.* I would then enter the company as a first year corps member during its metropolitan season in the spring of 2013. I was speechless upon hearing this news. Here was my dream, tantalising me like a chocolate ice-cream cone, and I had to watch it melt.

I suppose I could have tried to get out of my commitment to DTH, but my parents raised me with integrity, and I knew it wasn't the right thing to do. I decided to put my dreams of a classical company away for a while and audition with ABT again the following year.

I threw my heart and energy into DTH, determined to do my best for it during its 2012–2013 ballet season. I made friends among the dancers, and I learned so much from an artistic staff that I greatly admired.

While with the company, I had opportunities to visit places in the world that I never thought I would see. We travelled to Turkey and Israel.

While in Tel Aviv, I swam in the Mediterranean Sea for the first time in my life. Then we travelled across the country to Jerusalem. I felt a special link with my mother there. When she was in the third grade, her pen pal was from Israel. She had always longed to visit the country, but she never had the opportunity to go.

I felt like I was going in my mother's place. While at the Wailing Wall, I even left a prayer for her in the chinks of the wall, and I wore my *hamesh* (or *hamsa*), a handshaped charm, for protection during our travels to the Dome of the Rock and the salty Dead Sea.

Mom had insisted that I wear the *hamesh* she had given me. Muslims believe that it represents the hand of Fatima, the daughter of Mohammed, and Jews believe that it represents the hand of Miriam, the sister of Moses.

Mom explained to me that thousands of years ago, when the pharaoh was killing Jewish baby boys, Miriam had protected her baby brother, Moses, from the wrath of the pharaoh by floating him down the Nile River. He was then found by the pharaoh's wife and raised as a son of Egypt. Mom believed that when I wore the *hamesh*,

I would be protected, just like Moses had been. I simply believe that the *hamesh* represents my mother's hand, reaching out to protect me from half a world away.

Besides travelling to exotic lands, I had other wonderful experiences with DTH. I was cast in the role of the Black Swan, in an excerpt from *Swan Lake*, and I relished the chance to demonstrate my technique and grace as a classical dancer. This was a tough role, and I struggled with the artistry of it. It wasn't enough to perform a technically perfect dance. I needed to *become* the Black Swan, not just dance. I needed to seduce my partner, not merely flirt with him.

One review shook me up. The reviewer said that the Black Swan was trying to woo Prince Siegfried with her rock-solid technique.

'I think that's a wonderful review!' one of my friends at DTH told me. But I knew that it was a terrible review. I told myself that if I wanted to make it as a classical ballerina, I'd need to use my face as much as my feet. I needed to act as well as dance.

That night I stood in front of a mirror and danced the Black Swan. My arms and legs knew what to do. I didn't need to watch them. I focused on my face, especially my eyes. Then I told myself that a girl was trying to steal Skyler away from me.

My face transformed in front of my eyes. My nose flared, my eyes narrowed, and I realised that I looked like Odile. At my next performance, after hundreds of hours of practising to be the Black Swan, I finally became the Black Swan.

It was my last performance with DTH and my final performance of the season at the Jacob's Pillow Dance Festival. It was possibly my last performance in the United States for a long time. This performance was an epiphany, and the timing couldn't have been more perfect.

Chapter 36
Taking Flight

In December 2012, just six months before the Jacob's Pillow Dance Festival, I had auditioned with Het Nationale Ballet, also known as the Dutch National Ballet. This is one of the top classical companies in the world, so I thought that my chances of being invited to join were slim.

At the end of the audition, Ted Brandsen, the artistic director, came up to me smiling, but he didn't say a word. I was holding my breath. Finally I could no longer hold it. I exhaled loudly and gasped, 'Did I make it?'

'Of course. Why would you think that you didn't?' he asked.

How could I answer him? Could I say, 'Because I'm black'?

In my mind this invitation was of historical proportions. I felt that the hiring of a very black girl like me by one of the top classical ballet companies was akin to a white man's offering Rosa Parks a seat at the front of the bus in 1955! I happily signed the contract with the Dutch National Ballet in February.

Shortly after making my decision, I took three weeks off from touring with DTH so that I could return to South Africa and the South African Mzansi Ballet, which had recently been renamed the Joburg Ballet. This time I had no fears. I wasn't returning to a continent that held only terror for me. I was returning to beloved friends, colleagues and fans.

In March I danced the role of Kitri in the Joburg Ballet's production of *Don Quixote*. Kitri is a joyous and high-energy role. I returned from that performance exhausted but emotionally recharged.

In case I should forget that life was more than ballet, two very special invitations reminded me. I was invited to serve as a volunteer to the United Nations as a spokesperson for children affected by war, and I had the good fortune to be invited to participate in the 2013 Women in the World Conference at the Koch Theater at Lincoln Center. I was videotaped during an interview in which I had a chance to speak about my experiences as a child affected by war.

I opened the event with a dance, and my mother and I were interviewed on the stage about our experiences with international adoption. Then I sat down with my her and my sisters as we watched others on that stage tell their lives. I was deeply moved by the stories of women, many of them born into poverty and still remaining in poverty, who were finding ways to help others.

In late 2012, I was named by the *Huffington Post* as one of the '18 under 18: *HuffPost Teen*'s List of the Most Amazing Young People of the Year'. I didn't feel that I had done anything to deserve this. I couldn't imagine how I had managed to make that list, especially considering that I shared it with such incredible teens, like Malala Yousafzai, the Pakistani teen activist for the education of girls and women, who was shot for standing up to the Taliban, and Gabby Douglas, the African American young woman who won a gold medal in the Olympics.

Shortly afterwards, that honour was followed by others when, in 2013, I was named in 'Women in the World: 25 Under-25 Young Women to Watch' by the *Daily Beast*, and in the *Newsweek* list of '125 Women of Impact', and *O*'s '50 Things that Will Make You Say "Wow!"' Again, I was aligned with women whose backstories left me breathless with awe and respect for them.

As a result of all these honours and my recent hiring by a classical ballet company, I began to ponder my good fortune. I realised that it didn't just start in the past year. UNICEF estimates that there are three hundred and twenty thousand orphans in Sierra Leone, out of a population of approximately six million! Many more children died during the conflict. Only a very small group of children escaped during the height of the war. I was one of the lucky few. That seemed to be the key. Why was I one of the lucky ones?

'Mom, why did you and Daddy adopt? I'm not talking about adopting just me. Why did you adopt in the first place? Wouldn't you have had a lot more money if you only raised Adam and Erik?'

Without a long explanation, my mother simply said, 'We were blessed, and with blessing comes responsibility.' Well, I certainly knew that I was blessed. So I suppose that meant I had a responsibility . . . but to do what? That was the mystery that began plaguing me.

'A responsibility to do what?' I asked her.

'To share,' Mom answered.

'To share what?'

'You'll have to figure that out on your own,' she said.

I tried to think of what I had to share. I didn't have much money to my name, so I couldn't share wealth. I couldn't share my home, because I was already sharing a tiny New York City apartment bedroom with two sisters. I really didn't have anything material to share, other than a closet full of tutus, but I did have a lot of passion, drive, persistence and hope, especially hope. But how does someone share hope?

When my mother first suggested that I might want to write my memoir and offered to help me do it, I didn't see the point. 'I'm only seventeen,' I said. 'What could I possibly have to share in a memoir?'

Now I feel that I had a responsibility to write the memoir, and I saw what I had to share. In addition to all the rest of my blessings, I had been blessed with a hardy dose of hope. It was hope that enabled me to survive in Africa in the face of abuse, starvation, pain and terrible danger. It was hope that made me dare to dream, and it was hope that helped that dream take flight. Yes, I would share my hope.

Epilogue

My life was most profoundly impacted by two women. One is my wonderful mother, whose caring arms I walked into on that June day in 1999, when I arrived at the airport in Ghana.

The second woman is someone I had never met, yet she helped me get through my most terrible days in Sierra Leone and inspired me to be a ballerina. She is the ballerina on the cover of my magazine.

On the night before Mia and I left Africa with our new mother, there had been a blackout in Accra, the capital of Ghana. My mother had packed our bags in pitch-darkness, so she wasn't quite sure where everything was. 'My only concern was our money, our passports, and your orphan visas,' she later explained.

I was very sick at the airport, so she held me in her arms while she checked our bags and kept track of Mia. Twenty-four hours later, when we arrived at the John F. Kennedy International Airport in New York, we were one bag short. It wasn't until days later that my mother realised that the missing bag contained the picture of the ballerina and the clothes that we had worn in Sierra Leone.

I missed that picture, but eventually real ballet lessons replaced the promise that the picture had held for me. As the years went by, my mother and I searched the internet for my ballerina. Often Mom would have me pose for her so that she'd know what she was looking for.

One day Mom found her. She was on the cover of *Dance Magazine.* The image we downloaded was only postage-size, so we couldn't read the name of the ballerina, and weren't even sure of the date of publication. When Mom tried to enlarge it, the photo was just a blur, so I kept the tiny image as a memory.

Shortly before I left for Amsterdam to begin my contract with the Dutch National Ballet, a Dutch journalist named Steffie Kouters interviewed me for a magazine. During the interview I told her about the ballerina on the cover of the magazine and what she had meant to me.

Three months later Steffie called my mother and asked for a picture of the cover. Mom apologised for its size and quality, then sent it to her, and Steffie contacted *Dance Magazine.* She was able to get a copy of the cover from the publisher. Now we could see that the issue was dated May 1979. No wonder the magazine was so worn when I found it.

The ballerina on the cover was Magali Messac, who was a principal dancer with the Pennsylvania Ballet at the time. Coincidentally, that was the same company where I would dance as a Party Girl in *The Nutcracker* twenty-four years later. Eventually, Magali became a principal dancer at ABT, where I trained.

Steffie helped my mother track down Magali. My mother contacted my ballerina and discovered that she was very familiar with my story and had seen *First Position*. She had been moved by the story of the magazine and never dreamt that she was my ballerina. She was deeply touched to learn of the role that she played in my life, and she said that she wanted to give me her copy of the issue. I cried when my mother emailed me in Amsterdam and told me this.

By the time you read this book, Magali and I will have met. My heart pounds like an African drum at the thought of it. I hope that my mother will be present for our meeting. I would like to have my picture taken with the two women who changed my life for the better.

Acknowledgements

Most of all I want to thank my mother and father, Elaine and Charles DePrince, for their wisdom, sacrifice, love, support, encouragement and faith in me through the ups and downs of my life. I love you both so much!

I also wish to thank my birth parents for their belief that a girl child is just as good as a boy child, and for believing that girls deserve to go to school.

I thank the real Papa Andrew for sheltering me in his orphanage and bringing me to safety, and the real Uncle Sulaiman, who had the courage to beg for the life of 'a poor orphan pikin'.

Thank you, my dear sister Mia, for the love and friendship we have shared for so many years, in hardship and in joy. Let's not allow time or circumstance to get in the way of that.

I will be eternally grateful to Magali Messac, the ballerina on the cover of my magazine. Her smile and grace gave me hope for my future when I had nothing else.

I want to acknowledge the wonderful people at the Maine Adoption Placement Service, who worked to bring Mia, Mariel and me to America, and who continue to help families and rescue children all over the world.

I owe a debt of gratitude to a boy who died before I was born. My brother Michael, for whom I am named, insisted that my parents adopt 'a starving orphan from war-torn Africa'. Mom and Dad admitted that they might never have thought of it on their own. Michael, I wish I could give you a big hug.

Through my brother Teddy's kindness and generosity of spirit, I was able to overcome my fear of young men. I thank him, and will miss him always. I also thank all of the other members of my family for their love and affection, including brothers, sisters, sisters-in-law, brother-in-law, nieces and nephew. What a terrific family. I am so happy to have every single one of you in my life.

I want to thank Bo and Stephanie Spassoff, Arthur Mitchell, Mariaelena Ruiz, Charla Genn, Franco De Vita, Kate Lydon, Alaina Albertson-Murphy, Bill Glassman, Susan Jaffe, Natalya Zeiger, Raymond Lukens, and all of the other dedicated ballet teachers who have poured so much energy into my training.

I owe a special debt of gratitude to the artistic directors who had enough faith in me to invite me to dance with their companies. This includes Madeline Cantarella

Culpo, Virginia Johnson, Dirk Badenhorst, Ted Brandsen, Ernst Meisner, Kevin McKenzie and my 'Dutch papas', Rinus Sprong and Thom Stuart, who introduced me to the Netherlands.

I certainly cannot forget Bess Kargman. I'm so glad that you had the persistence to follow me around and the courage to expose issues of race in ballet. I am honoured to be a part of *First Position*, which has affected my life in such a positive way.

I am grateful to my friends all over the world who have encouraged me through the years, but especially to the boy who fell in love with me, my beloved Skyler MaxeyWert.

Mom, again, I can't thank you enough. Not only did you love me, raise me, instil strong values in me, and teach me to cook, but you also taught me to write those five-paragraph essays and you co-authored this book with me.

And last, but certainly not least, I cannot thank enough the people who believed in this memoir: my literary agent, Adriana Dominguez; my editor, Erin Clarke; all of the people on my Random House team; and my enthusiastic editors worldwide, who've made it possible for this book to reach readers in so many countries and languages.

I feel blessed to have had each and every one of you in my life.

Picture Credits

All photographs are reproduced courtesy of Elaine and Michaela DePrince, with the exception of:

First Position movie poster: courtesy of Bess Kargman c/o United Talent Agency

Dancing with the Stars © American Broadcasting Companies, Inc./Peter 'Hopper' Stone

Michaela as the Black Swan in *Swan Lake* with the Dance Theatre of Harlem: photograph by Rachel Neville, with kind permission of the Dance Theatre of Harlem

Dance Magazine cover: courtesy of Jacob's Pillow Dance Festival archive

Michaela in *Le Corsaire* with the Joburg Ballet: with kind permission of the Joburg Ballet

Every effort has been made to contact all copyright holders. The publishers would be pleased to rectify at the earliest opportunity any omissions or errors brought to their notice.